PAYING FOR COLLEGE

PAYING FOR COLLEGE

A GUIDE FOR PARENTS

GERALD KREFETZ

College Entrance Examination Board
New York

In all of its book publishing activities the College Board endeavors to present the works of authors who are well qualified to write with authority on the subject at hand, and to present accurate and timely information. However, the opinions, interpretations, and conclusions of the authors are their own and do not necessarily represent those of the College Board; nothing contained herein should be assumed to represent an official position of the College Board, or any of its members.

Copies of this book may be ordered from College Board Publications, Box 886, New York, New York 10101-0886. The price is $14.

Editorial inquiries concerning this book should be directed to Editorial Office, The College Board, 45 Columbus Avenue, New York, New York 10023-6992.

Library of Congress Catalog Number: 94-069940
ISBN: 0-87447-439-6

Printed in the United States of America

9 8 7 6 5 4 3 2 1

CONTENTS

1 PLANNING TO MEET COLLEGE COSTS   **1**

COLLEGE AND THE ECONOMY   1
THE PURPOSE OF PLANNING   4
    Family Contribution   4
    Need Analysis   5
    Methodology   6
    Financial Aid   7
    The Importance of Saving   7

2 FACTS ABOUT SAVING   **11**

COLLEGE COSTS   11
THE SAVINGS GAP AND COLLEGE   13
THE COMPLEXITIES OF SAVING   14
ASSESSING RISKS AND REWARDS   18
HOW MUCH SHOULD YOU SAVE   18

3 INSTRUMENTS OF SAVINGS   21

FINANCIAL INSTRUMENTS   21
SAVINGS ACCOUNTS   22
NOW AND SUPER-NOW ACCOUNTS   24
MONEY-MARKET DEPOSIT ACCOUNTS   26
CERTIFICATES OF DEPOSIT   28
MONEY-MARKET FUNDS   30
U.S. SAVINGS BONDS   32
TREASURY BILLS, NOTES, AND BONDS   35
GOVERNMENT AGENCY SECURITIES   37
MORTGAGE-BACKED SECURITIES   39
ZERO-COUPON BONDS (TREASURIES)   41
ZERO-COUPON BONDS (MUNICIPALS AND CORPORATES)   43
MUNICIPAL BONDS   45
CORPORATE BONDS   48
COMMON STOCKS   50
INSURANCE   52

4 GIFTS   55

THE ROLE OF GIFTS   55
INHERITANCES   56
EXAMPLES OF GIFTS   57
THE UNIFORM GIFTS TO MINORS ACT   60
BORROWBACK REVISITED   64

5 TAXES AND INCOME SHIFTING   67

CHILDREN UNDER 14   70
CHILDREN OVER 14   72

6 TRUSTS AND LOANS   73

MINORS TRUST [2503 (c) TRUST]   75
THE CLIFFORD TRUST   77
THE CRUMMEY TRUST   79
CHARITABLE-REMAINDER TRUST   80

7 BUSINESS AND COLLEGE
COSTS   81

HIRE YOUR CHILD   81
EDUCATIONAL FRINGE BENEFITS   83
CHILDREN AS PARTNERS   85
S CORPORATIONS AND ORDINARY CORPORATIONS 87
BUSINESS GIFTS AND LEASEBACKS   89
BORROWING FROM YOUR RETIREMENT PLAN   90
  Individual Retirement Account   91
  Keogh Plans   92
  401 (k) or Salary-Reduction Plans   93

8 BORROWING   95

PAY-AS-YOU-GO   95
LINES OF CREDIT   97
HOME EQUITY LOANS   99
MARGIN ACCOUNTS   101
HIGHER EDUCATION AMENDMENTS OF 1992   102
COLLEGE LOAN AND TUITION PROGRAMS   103
  Loan Programs   104
  Tuition Plans   106
  Tuition Bonds   108
  Federal Stafford Loans   109

Loans for Parents   110
Federal Direct Student Loan Program   111
Federal Perkins Loan Program   111
Miscellaneous Loan Sources   112

9   TAILORING FINANCIAL STRATEGIES TO PERSONAL CIRCUMSTANCES   113

PROFILE 1: YOUNG FAMILY   114
PROFILE 2: DIVORCED MOTHER   116
PROFILE 3: YOUNG PROFESSIONALS, TWO INCOMES   118
PROFILE 4: WIDOWED FATHER, INDEPENDENT
    BUSINESSMAN   120
PROFILE 5: INDEPENDENT PROFESSIONALS   121
PROFILE 6: GRANDPARENTS AND ORPHANED
    GRANDCHILDREN   123
FACTS TO KEEP IN MIND   125

APPENDIX A: 1994 TAX RATE SCHEDULES   127
APPENDIX B: GIFT TAX TABLE   129
APPENDIX C: INCOME TAX RATE SCHEDULE FOR TRUSTS   130
APPENDIX D: INTEREST RATES AND YIELDS   131
APPENDIX E: WORKSHEETS AND TABLES   133

GLOSSARY   141
INDEX   149

PAYING FOR COLLEGE

1

PLANNING TO MEET COLLEGE COSTS

COLLEGE AND THE ECONOMY

This book is written for families that expect to pay most, if not all, of the costs of college out of savings, investments, gifts, inheritances, borrowed funds, or a combination of those sources. It outlines the customary ways of financing a college education, but it also indicates some unorthodox methods that may prove useful. It is of paramount importance to scan every legitimate option and rethink strategy. Rising costs and the likelihood of rising taxes make it imperative to take advantage of all available benefits, whether they be in financial aid, grants, or scholarships. Families should start as early as possible to develop appropriate investment and savings plans to help pay the freight.

The balance of the 1990s is likely to be quite different from the 1980s as low inflation and slow growth replace an expansive boom, rising prices, and growing assets. As cautious economic times displace an era of unlimited exuberance, it is important for the consumer of college education to be especially vigilant in obtaining the best value for hard-earned funds.

1

While the economic scene may appear grim for the time being, there are some silver linings to consider. Demographically, in response to the baby boom of the 1970s and 1980s, educational institutions expanded their facilities and staffs to accommodate expanded student enrollment. To a large degree, coping with the baby boomers created a tidal wave of educational inflation. Throughout the 1980s, college costs rose an average of 7 percent per year. With the reduction of the demographic bulge, those rapid cost increases may soon be history.

Moreover, the 1990–92 economic recession has created a period of plentiful credit. Lenders may be more cautious in lending money, but when they do, it will likely be at far lower rates of interest than were considered normal in the 1980s.

Lower interest rates are something of a two-edged sword. While one may be able to obtain funds at lower rates (certainly a plus for borrowers), interest paid to savers is also much reduced—a significant negative factor. As the recession began, 14 percent of family income came from interest earned on their savings. With many interest rates cut in half in the 1990–92 recession, family income has correspondingly shrunk. And with the shrinking of real estate values, many Americans now feel poorer.

Recessions and periods of slow growth also have an insidious psychological effect. It seems that economic good times will never reappear. With pessimism ascendant, it is sometimes hard to see the forest for the trees, hard to believe that a college education is worthwhile, let alone achievable. Can the large costs and significant sacrifices be justified in view of the problematic outlook for the economy?

Business cycles have been a constant in Western economies for over 200 years—and nothing on the horizon suggests that the cyclical nature of the economy has changed. The pattern has been that just about the time when everyone is saying that "it is different this time," the pall lifts and the economy revives.

No doubt college costs will continue to be expensive, to make major demands on family resources, regardless of the economic weather. But there should be little question as to the value of higher education, both financially and intellectually.

Whether college pays, in the last analysis, is a very personal judgment for parents and children, one based on cultural, social, and psychological considerations. A college education clearly cannot be valued only for its potential earning power in life. A broadened mind, a more tolerant outlook, a somewhat more sophisticated understanding of one's own and others' behavior, an acquired skill, a sharpened intellect, a surfaced talent, are all part and parcel of a successful education. The financial value of a college education is fairly self-evident. Its value is doubly enhanced by the economic restructuring presently being forced on the country by foreign competition and global marketing. America has always been in the lead in terms of industrial productivity, but that is now being challenged. Moreover, there is a shift to a postindustrial society: the fastest growing sector of the economy is now the service area. To maintain parity with the rest of the world, and simply to keep up a standard of living comparable to the previous generation, Americans will be obliged to work hard and smarter, if not longer.

Heretofore, higher education was considered a transitional stage while students considered which direction to take. It is still that, but it has also taken on a pragmatic overtone, a preparatory waystation in the serious business of earning a living.

Besides the rising level of international competition and educational attainment, domestic competition has intensified. About one-third of the population under 35 years of age has completed four years of college—not too long ago it was only 10 percent. And no doubt the numbers will escalate as the year 2000 nears and government focuses on educational goals for the next century and methods of reaching them.

There is a strong correlation between educational attainment and income achievements. Put quite simply, the longer a student remains in school, the higher his or her income is likely to be when formal education is completed. While it sometimes takes a few years for a college graduate to catch up to the high school graduate who has been in the work force, there is little question that the college graduate will make far more money throughout a working career.

How much more? In general terms for men, about 45 percent more, and about 59 percent more with a postgraduate degree. For women, a college degree will mean earnings 25 percent higher than for those with a high school diploma, or 77 percent more for a woman with a postgraduate degree. To put it somewhat differently, the average net worth of a household with only a high school diploma is $109,000, but a household with a college degree has a net worth of $364,600.

Unequivocally, college pays! Of course, college tuition is no small cost and that, too, must be placed in the equation. Nevertheless, current evidence suggests that the observation of the Department of Education a decade ago still holds true: "Over the long term . . . the financial returns of a college education may repay the actual costs of schooling, as well as the wages lost by not working during college years."

Indeed, in the current economic restructuring and highly competitive environment, the differentials between skilled and unskilled work are likely to grow rather than shrink. While this may have some disturbing social consequences, it behooves the individual and/or family to consider the costs of college a necessary expense for a more complete and satisfying life.

THE PURPOSE OF PLANNING

Family Contribution

Going to college is expensive. It is expensive to operate institutions of higher learning and that, in turn, makes it expensive to attend those institutions, though few colleges charge students the full costs of the services they provide and many parents and students pay only a portion of the stated costs. Nevertheless, since the family is considered the primary source of funds for college and is expected to pay its fair share of the cost of a college education, it is important to understand how that fair share is determined and how to accumulate the money to cover it.

First of all, how much will college cost? The following table is nothing more than a projection based on a 6 percent average annual rate of inflation. Quite possibly, it overstates the case: if inflation can be lowered to 3 percent, the approximate level at the time of this book's publication, then the real figures may be considerably lower. Nevertheless, it is advisable to base your savings and investment strategies on the higher inflation rate to be prepared for an unexpected rise that could affect the cost of your child's college education:

Table 1.1. The cost of a college education

Your child's age	Number of years until he/she enters college	Cost of 4-year public college education	Cost of 4-year private college education
15	3 years	$28,594	$75,043
13	5 years	$32,128	$84,318
11	7 years	$36,099	$94,740
9	9 years	$40,561	$106,450
7	11 years	$45,574	$119,607
5	13 years	$51,207	$134,391
3	15 years	$57,536	$151,001
1	17 years	$64,648	$169,665

It was recognized many years ago that a college education was expensive—too expensive for many families. It was also recognized that government (at all levels) had a special role in financing education, to make it available to all, regardless of resources.

Consequently, over the years, a number of programs were developed to provide general assistance. The role of government in education is an old one—perhaps best epitomized in the establishment of land-grant colleges in the nineteenth century.

Financial assistance is now well-entrenched in the nation's college funding system. It is, in essence, no different from other government programs, such as Social Security, Medicare, or Head Start. No doubt some individuals feel reluctant about applying for financial aid: however, it is funded by your income tax dollars and is a reflection of the importance attached to education. Since government is the prime cause of inflation, it is perhaps only just that it compensate the public, which has been hurt through rising prices, by pumping some funds back into the system.

Need Analysis

The precise portion of the total college bill to be picked up by a family depends on a number of factors that vary from family to family. Among them are the parents' income; the student's earning; the family's net assets; as well as the family's expenses. To determine the parents' estimated contribution and the student's eligibility for financial aid, all of these factors are subjected to the process of "need analysis," which also takes into consideration the parents' need to protect a portion of their assets for their retirement. The older a primary wage earner is, the larger the asset protection allowance is.

Methodology

To determine the extent of the assistance required, financial aid administrators use a formula determined by the federal government, better known as the Federal Methodology. This formula takes into consideration earned income, unearned income, assets, expenses, family size, age, and other factors. In recent years the Federal Methodology has been liberalized—some financial factors are no longer used in the formulation of defining need.

Consequently, some colleges have applied more restrictive definitions in determining need, informally known as the Institutional Methodology. Colleges that use the Institutional Methodology are attempting to obtain a more comprehensive picture of a family's finances.

In brief, there are a few differences, but the net result may lead to significantly different aid packages. Therefore, you should be aware of which methodology a school is basing its definition of need on. The Federal Methodology does *not* consider the value of a family's home in tallying a family's assets. Moreover, the income of a divorced, noncustodial parent is *not* included in a tally of income. The Institutional Methodology *does* include the value of a family's home and *does* require information on the income of a noncustodial parent.

The Institutional Methodology is likely to diminish the aid award, while the Federal Methodology is likely to enhance it. Under the federal formula there is virtually no possibility of negotiation and little college discretion in the award. The institutional approach gives a school wider discretion, and the first offer of assistance is not necessarily the last and/or optimum offer.

While there is no typical need analysis example, Table 1.2 indicates very approximately what the expected parental contribution might be under the Federal Methodology for a two-parent family with two children, one in college, based on annual incomes ranging from $20,000 to $60,000. An abbreviated analysis for one

**Table 1.2. Relationship of family income to parental
contribution (1993–94 Federal Methodology)**

Annual family income	Net income (after tax)	Parents' contribution (annual)	Percentage of total	Percentage of net
$20,000	$16,150	$ 40	0.2	0.2
25,000	19,618	800	3.2	4.1
30,000	23,085	1,560	5.2	6.8
35,000	26,553	2,360	6.7	8.9
40,000	30,020	3,320	8.3	11.1
45,000	33,488	4,540	10.1	13.6
50,000	36,955	6,070	12.1	16.4
55,000	39,903	7,450	13.5	18.7
60,000	42,999	8,910	14.9	20.7

Note: Estimated parents' contributions assume four family members; one family member in college as an undergraduate; older parent (age 45) is employed; the other parent is not employed; income only from employment; no unusual circumstances; standard deductions on U.S. income tax; asset neutrality (assets equal to Asset Protection Allowance). Values are approximate. Table prepared by the College Scholarship Service.

such family might look like the one in Table 1.3. This analysis uses the Federal Methodology; under the Institutional Methodology, the family might be expected to contribute more to college costs.

Many families would find it challenging to pay $2,000 out of current income, which underscores the importance of having savings to draw on to cover college costs. These calculations do not mean that a family in similar circumstances must consider only colleges that cost around $2,000. Many families, even those with fairly high incomes, cannot pay the full cost of a college education by themselves. For those who qualify, financial aid is available to help meet such direct costs as tuition, fees, books, and related personal expenses such as food, housing, and transportation.

Financial Aid

Financial aid comes from several sources, the primary ones being the federal government, state governments, colleges, and private programs. There are three kinds of financial aid:

- Grants or scholarships that do not have to be repaid. Grants are usually based on need alone. Scholarships may be based on need and/or outstanding accomplishment.

- Loans that must be repaid. Loan programs sponsored by the federal government, state agencies, or colleges often have lower interest rates than commercial loans and may defer repayment until after graduation.

- Work-student programs that provide earnings from part-time jobs during the academic year. These are usually arranged for students by the college.

Table 1.3

Income	
Parents' income	$35,000
Other income (dividends, interest, etc.)	500
Total income	$35,500
Expenses	
Income taxes (federal, state)	$ 6,247
Social security taxes	$ 2,678
Employment allowance	0
Income protection allowance	$17,150
Total allowance against income	$26,785
Available income	$ 8,715
Assets	
Equity in real estate other than the home	0
Business or farm	0
Cash, savings, and checking accounts	$ 2,500
Other investments	0
Total assets	$ 2,500
Deductions	
Asset Protection Allowance	$44,100
Remaining assets (APA subtracted from total assets)	($41,600)
Income supplement from assets	0
Adjusted available income	$ 8,715
Parents' Expected Contribution	$ 1,917

Most aid is based on demonstrated need, which is generally defined as the difference between what it costs to attend a college and what a family can contribute to that cost. This means that the amount of aid can vary depending on the institution. It is probable that a higher priced private institution may be able to provide a larger aid package than that offered by a lower priced public institution. Therefore families should not rule out higher cost colleges without investigating whether they are eligible for financial aid. For example, in the case of the family cited above with an annual earned income of $35,000, the student's financial aid package might be that shown in Table 1.4 for a college costing $13,000 a year.

One useful free source of information about financial aid is *The Student Guide,* a pamphlet published by the U.S. Department of Education. It can be ordered by mail from Federal Student Aid Programs, P.O. Box 84, Washington, DC 20044, or by phone at 1-800-433-3243. An excellent source of detailed, annually up-dated information about financial aid and specific costs at nearly 3,000 colleges and universities is *College Costs and Financial Aid Handbook.* Published by the College Board, the current edition is $16.00. An interactive software program, *College Cost Explorer FUND FINDER,* also published by the College Board and available in many high schools and public libraries, provides comparable information for computer users. It offers the added advantages of electronic worksheets for speedy automatic calculations and a data base of approximately 3,000 scholarship programs.

Since financial aid is intended as a supplement, however, parents must think of themselves as the primary source of college

Table 1.4

Parents' contribution	$1,917
College costs	$13,000
Financial need	$11,083
Financial aid	
College scholarship	$ 3,000
State scholarship	$ 2,000
Federal Stafford Loan	$ 2,625
Federal PLUS Loan	$ 1,375
Federal Work-Study	$ 2,083
Total financial aid award	$11,083

funds. Therefore, families should start as early as possible to plan for the costs of higher education.

THE IMPORTANCE OF SAVING

Families with little or no savings find it difficult, if not impossible, to pay for college expenses out of current income. No matter how large your income is, without advance planning college costs may represent a prohibitively high outlay. Only long-term planning can significantly ease the burden of paying college costs and enable parents and students to avoid the drain on future income resulting from loan repayments.

The daunting sum of four years' tuition, room, board, and related expenses can be manageable if a family has saved and invested regularly. The key factor is setting realistic goals and fulfilling them. This book offers information about a wide range of options for achieving those goals.

2

FACTS ABOUT SAVING

**An investment in knowledge
pays the best interest.**
Benjamin Franklin, 1758

COLLEGE COSTS

The annual national survey of college costs by College Board for 1993–94 found that college tuition and fees rose between 6 and 10 percent. This compared (unfavorably) to a rise of about 3 to 4 percent for the consumer price index (CPI). Clearly, inflation in college costs outpaced the general price structure—a trend over a decade old.

In concrete terms, the survey found that students at four-year private colleges paid $11,025 for tuition and fees (a 6 percent increase), and $6,175 (a 7 percent increase) at two-year colleges. At in-state public institutions, the average for tuition and fees at four-year colleges was $2,527 (up by 8 percent), and $1,229 (up by 10 percent) at two-year colleges.

Both sets of figures omit room and board. The average expense for room and board at four-year institutions was $4,793 at private colleges and $3,680 at public colleges. In brief, an average private college was charging $15,818 and at a public college the

tab was $6,207 for one year of study. Of course, extras ranging
from textbooks to transportation can increase the overall cost by
one or two thousand dollars.

Such prices are enough to cause "sticker shock" to parents,
and consternation to students. And as tuition, fees, room, and
board escalate each year, there are gloomy prophecies about future costs. The prospects are indeed cause for concern. One prom-
inent money management company projects that in 18 years
today's newborn faces a bill at a top four-year private institution
of $275,824, or $125,884 at one of the costliest public colleges.
Of course, average prices, as seen in the first chapter, will be
considerably lower. Should inflation continue to abate, they may
go still lower.

But extrapolating trends is a dangerous business, and as the
famous biologist René Dubos once said, "present trends never
continue."

Regardless of the exact tuition charges in 5, 10, or 15 years,
the likelihood is that more of the increases are going to be shoul-
dered by parents and students. The national government does
indeed provide assistance for a substantial number of college students. But that assistance has provided less and less actual help
when adjusted for inflation, and many middle-income parents
believe that they will be hard pressed to put two or three children
through college. Nevertheless, it is possible to afford college tuition without declaring bankruptcy or moving to the poorhouse.
Government assistance may not have kept pace with increases in
college costs, but there is still substantial aid available.

Pell grants are an important source, accounting for some 18
percent of student aid. By far the largest single source in recent
years, however, is the Federal Family Education Loans Program,
which includes Stafford Loans and Parents Loans for Undergraduate Students (PLUS). In 1992–93, that program provided 43
percent of available aid. Those forms of assistance, when combined with family savings and investment plans, make college a
feasible proposition.

Remember, the federal government presently contributes
over $25 billion to various educational programs, and the states
provide hundreds of millions more, as do a wide range of corporations, membership organizations, and foundations. The bulk of
those funds is distributed on a need-based, first come, first served
basis, but there are times when not all monies are actually spent,

because of unmet eligibility requirements. With the number of financial assistance packages, loans of all kinds, work-study programs, scholarships, plus private investment and savings, there is no reason that a college education should be denied to anyone.

THE SAVINGS GAP AND COLLEGE

Saving for college, or for anything else, used to be a simple matter. All the textbooks suggested that a set percentage of income after taxes be saved. The advice was reasonable and simple. Average Americans could save 5 or 6 percent of their disposable income. And most citizens placed their savings on deposit with a savings bank, commercial bank, credit union, or savings and loan association. The standard rate of interest for their deposits was 5.25 or 5.5 percent.

Those simple days have vanished due to a number of tumultuous political and economic events over the past two decades. The central issue in the seventies and eighties was inflation. The consumer price index went from 41 in 1971 to 138 in 1991—an increase of more than 300 percent in 20 years. Typical consumers were not as lucky because their earning power did not keep up. The median income of families remained relatively stable: In 1971 they earned $27,500, while in 1991 they earned $36,000, an increase of not quite 30 percent. What made the slide in purchasing power tolerable was the great increase of two-income families as spouses entered the work force.

While many families have more income because there are two wage earners, the cost of higher education has continued to increase. Clearly, parents must use every device and technique available in order to close the college cost gap. With the average public college tuition and board bills in excess of $6,000 per year and the private college $15,818, college costs can run between 25 and 50 percent of an average one-income household's after-tax income.

Even two-income families are likely to be seriously burdened by such expenditures, especially if more than one family member attends college, particularly if they are in college at the same time. Most families receive some sort of tuition assistance in the form of grants, loans, scholarships, and tuition-assistance programs.

Sixty-three percent of all students at private schools receive some form of aid, while 31 percent receive aid at public colleges. Therefore, it is imperative to understand the fundamentals of saving for college. Grants, scholarships, tuition-assistance programs, and loans may all help, and certainly should not be neglected in a total financial package, but unless a family has started a college savings program, the other bricks will not have a foundation on which to rest. Beginning early to save regularly is a sound approach for families at every income level.

THE COMPLEXITIES OF SAVING

Saving money is no longer as simple as it used to be. Economic forces have brought about substantial changes in monetary and fiscal policies, the administration of taxes, level of debts, and the art of investing. The act of saving is now complicated since it involves a multitude of other financial choices—questions of diversification, safety of principal, liquidity, maturity of debt instruments, estate planning, legal ownership—and a host of other issues, such as inflation and deflation, which must be considered to stay abreast of the game, let alone ahead of it.

The most fundamental event to affect savers in recent years was the deregulation of the financial world. After more than a decade of inflation, the rigidities of the financial system imposed by the Federal Reserve System had created an impossible situation. Regulations passed in the 1930s to protect the banking system from too much competition limited the amount of interest banks could pay depositors on time deposits. As long as interest rates did not generally exceed those levels, these limits posed no problem. However, in the 1970s interest rates started to exceed those levels because of inflation. Lenders wished to be compensated for the loss of future purchasing power. Or, to put it in financial terms, lenders had to be protected from the ravages of a depreciating currency if they were to be induced to lend.

Lenders, or depositors of financial institutions, saw their interest income not only shrink but disappear in real terms. One measure of inflation used by economists is the "implicit price deflator for the gross national product"—a measurement of average change in market prices of goods and services compared to average levels in a base period. By this indicator, annual change in prices first exceeded 5.1 percent in 1969. Thus, prices were increasing as fast as the interest rates banks could legally pay depositors—5 or 5.25 percent. In real terms, the savers and/or lenders were on a treadmill. In fact, depositors who lent their funds to a bank were really beginning to fall behind in the late sixties since their earned interest was taxable. If depositors were in the 20 percent bracket, a nominal 5 percent interest rate on their deposits left only 4 percent after taxes.

It was then that savers and lenders realized that inflation was causing them to fall behind. Between the fixed ceiling on interest-rate deposits that the government had mandated and the effect of taxation, the real return on their savings was decidedly negative.

Furthermore, free-market interest rates were climbing in order to reflect the negative effects of inflation. While the government could set interest rates for small depositors, it was long realized that it would be virtually impossible to fix interest rates on large sums. If the government were to sell or auction its massive debt obligations in the open market, rates would be set by supply and demand of funds. The government could occasionally lean against the wind by controlling the money supply, but in a free economy there was very little it could do to dictate interest rates.

Free-market interest rates quickly surpassed the regulated rates of the banks. While three-month Treasury bills sold to yield 3 and 4 percent per annum in the sixties, by 1969 the average yield was over 6.66 percent. That rate dropped somewhat in 1971 and 1972, but ratcheted ahead for the rest of the seventies. Treasury bills eventually topped out in May 1981 with a record yield of 16.29 percent.

Savers started to show their dissatisfaction at this reversal of values. Government regulations and taxation were penalizing them for keeping their monies in banks. When the tolls are too high, people will go out of their way to avoid paying them. So, too, in the 1970s, as savers scrambled to escape the financial pincers. It was the small savers who bore the brunt of these old regulations, since they were unable to purchase government debt obligations—Treasury bills, notes, and bonds. These instruments were sold in denominations beginning with $10,000, effectively locking small savers out of the higher, free-market yields.

The road around the tollbooth was pioneered by a new type of mutual fund—money-market funds. Instead of being composed of stocks and/or bonds, the underlying assets of these new funds were short-term debt instruments:

- Government bills—discounted Treasury bills that mature within 90, 180, or 360 days

- Banker's acceptances—bills of exchange drawn on a bank to pay specific bills for customers when the bills come due

- Commercial paper—unsecured short-term (less than 270 days) promissory notes of first-class corporations that are sold to corporate or individual investors

- Certificates of deposit—negotiable or transferable receipts that bear interest on funds deposited with a bank

The money-market funds grew in small amounts—the minimum purchase by the general public was $500 or $1,000. This money, after nominal administrative costs had been deducted, was then used to buy a portfolio of the above-mentioned debt instruments. In order to simplify the bookkeeping, each depositor or shareholder was issued shares that were denominated at $1. Money-market funds kept rolling over their debt instruments as they reached their maturity dates, that is, they reinvested their proceeds in similar debt paper. The interest and the yield from the discounted instruments were credited to the portfolio. Each fund varied its techniques, but in general the maturity of the portfolio was kept relatively short. Short-maturity paper of high quality kept almost all these funds out of trouble arising from credit problems of the underlying assets. However, these money-market funds did not have any government-backed insurance, even though a substantial part of their portfolio might consist of Treasury paper.

From a drop in the bucket in the early seventies, the money-market funds spread rapidly. A new cry was heard in the land—"disintermediation"—the removal of time deposits from the regulated depository institutions and the switching of them into the new funds. At first it was a trickle of funds leaving the nation's banking system, but as the seventies wore on the trickle became a river and the river a flood. As interest rates rose higher, American banks were being drained of liquidity.

By 1982 these funds had captured $200 billion of deposits, or one out of eight dollars that depositors had accumulated in small-time deposits.

In the late seventies bankers throughout the country raised a cry for a "level playing field" so that they could compete with the money-market funds. Pressure built for the deregulation of the financial world. Airlines, railroads, and telephone and trucking industries were already in the midst of deregulation. It was apropos for the banks as well.

In 1980 Congress made a major reform in the banking system by passing the Depository Institutions Deregulation and Monetary Control Act (DIDMCA). It gave the banking world what it so desperately needed—relief from mandated low interest rates. The act was hailed as the most significant banking legislation since the reforms of the thirties, or perhaps even since the 1913 Federal Reserve Act, which established central banking in this country. DIDMCA authorized the phasing out of interest-rate limitation on accounts held by depository institutions. It was accomplished in stages, and by the spring of 1986 the cumbersome controls on interest rates were totally deregulated.

This process of deregulation has not been without its dangers, but on the whole it has given the average saver a wider selection of savings accounts and savings instruments, more flexibility in managing money, and more interest income on his or her principal. But as commercial banks and thrifts (savings and loan associations, mutual savings banks, and credit unions) have become free to compete, they have also raised their fee structures. This has been something of a mixed blessing, especially for low-income families and those who make marginal use of banking facilities.

The 1980 act was followed by another equally significant law for savers—the Garn–St Germain Depository Institutions Act—which finally allowed commercial banks and savings and loan associations to offer money-market deposit accounts. Indeed, the authorization wording called for money-market deposit accounts that were to be "directly equivalent to and competitive with money-market mutual funds." The tollgates were finally lifted and in December 1982, approximately 80 percent of all the nation's banking institutions started money-market deposit accounts. These accounts were meant to go toe-to-toe with the money-market funds, and within a few months they went from zero to over $350 billion of deposits, exceeding the money-market funds.

Money-market deposit accounts were an immediate success with the savings public. They enabled everyone, not just the more sophisticated and wealthier saver who for a number of years had been using the funds for premium yields, to enjoy free-market rates. While the rates of money-market funds and money-market deposit accounts are similar, it should be appreciated that there are some basic differences (see Chapter 3).

ASSESSING RISKS AND REWARDS

It is important for families, particularly those with college-bound children, to obtain the highest rates of interest, the greatest yields, and the largest gains on their hard-earned dollars. Deregulation of the financial world became a reality in spring 1986, and depository institutions and financial-service organizations will continue to fabricate a number of new products to entice consumers and savers. While one should take advantage of whatever the marketplace has to offer, security, peace of mind, and the preservation of capital are as important as high yields.

Caution must continue to be the password: Any time high "teaser" interest rates or incredible opportunities are being touted, the red warning flag should be raised. Savers in dozens of savings and loan associations in Ohio, Maryland, and Rhode Island succumbed to deregulated wheeler-dealers. So while the deregulated market does offer new opportunities, it also offers greater risks. Savers for college educations, who are attempting to accumulate funds for what may well be their greatest single lifetime investment, must take advantage of this brave new world while practicing caution and restraint. It is perhaps a contradictory combination, but increasingly parents and children will move to shoulder a greater and greater portion of college costs. The least they must do is be aware of all the techniques and devices for financing a college education.

HOW MUCH SHOULD YOU SAVE?

The obvious answer to the question of how much to save is, as much as possible! Whether it be 5 percent of disposable income or (preferably) 5 percent of gross income, is a judgment of per-

| Age of oldest child now | To accumulate these amounts* by age 18 | | | | | | | | |
| | $10,000 | $20,000 | $30,000 | $40,000 | $50,000 | $75,000 | $100,000 | $125,000 | $150,000 |
	Set aside these monthly amounts								
1	$26	52	79	105	131	196	262	327	392
2	$29	58	87	116	145	217	290	362	454
3	$32	64	96	129	161	241	321	402	482
4	$36	72	107	143	179	269	358	448	537
5	$40	80	120	160	201	301	401	501	602
6	$45	90	135	181	226	339	452	564	677
7	$51	102	154	205	256	384	512	640	768
8	$58	117	175	234	292	438	585	731	877
9	$67	135	202	270	337	506	674	843	1,011
10	$79	157	236	315	394	590	787	984	1,181
11	$93	187	280	373	467	700	933	1,167	1,400
12	$113	226	339	452	565	847	1,129	1,411	1,694
13	$140	281	421	562	702	1,053	1,405	1,756	2,107
14	$182	364	546	728	910	1,364	1,819	2,274	2,729
15	$251	502	754	1,005	1,256	1,884	2,512	3,141	3,769

* Based on a fixed 7% interest rate, compounded monthly, and assuming no fluctuation in value of principal. No adjustment has been made for income taxes.
Source: The Franklin Group of Funds

sonal priorities. It is quite conceivable that you may not be able to save enough to cover the total cost of a four-year educational package. While that might be an appealing goal, it may not be practical or suitable to your lifestyle. If it is more realistic to set a lower goal, so be it. Perhaps what is most important is to get into the habit of saving.

If you initially attempt to save half of what the college bill will be, you are off to a good start. Loans, grants, scholarships, work-study, summer jobs are keys to paying the second half of the bill. Moreover, as age and career both advance, you will no doubt have additional funds for saving.

The table on page 19 will give you some idea of what sums are required on a monthly basis to accumulate the principal amounts. It is based on an 7.0 percent fixed interest rate, compounded monthly. No provision has been made for the payment of income tax.

3

INSTRUMENTS OF SAVINGS

FINANCIAL INSTRUMENTS

This book examines a number of ways to prepare for college costs—among them gifts, loans, trusts, family employment, and business arrangements. Because a key ingredient in almost all of these plans is the ability to save and invest wisely, and to begin doing so on a regular basis as early as possible, it is imperative to understand the wide range of possibilities open to the average parent and planner.

Since deregulation of the financial world by congressional acts, the consumer is faced with a new supermarket of financial products. This presents a potentially confusing array of choices, from adjustable-rate insurance policies to zero-coupon bonds, from risky high-yielding junk bonds to secure low-yielding passbook savings accounts.

This chapter is not an investment primer, but it does attempt to clarify some of the trustworthy and conventional ways of saving and investing, bearing in mind that security and the conservation of capital are foremost for savers. Most parents start to prepare for their children's college education later rather than sooner. This naturally reduces their flexibility in handling their resources and in taking full advantage of some of the previously mentioned techniques. Nevertheless, the following section includes both short-term and long-term methods of accumulating monies. While savings are an important part of a financial plan, it is important to consider a range of investments to complement the predictable stream of earnings arising from saving.

Savings Accounts

Definition

Old habits die hard and most Americans before 1980 knew of no other saving mechanism than the passbook savings account. The day of the passbook savings account with fixed interest rates has passed, but not everyone has gotten the word, since billions of savings are still held in low-interest-bearing accounts.

While passbook savings accounts were a traditional way of introducing children to the virtues of saving, they are assuredly a poor choice for saving for a child's education. At best they should be used for short-term, small-ticket goals. They will undoubtedly remain popular for Christmas Clubs and other forced savings for an immediate purpose.

Passbook savings accounts are still available at most depository institutions. They are easy accounts to open, usually require one's presence to deposit or withdraw (though it is possible to use the mails), but cannot be used to make payments to third parties. Interest is relatively low, about 4 percent, but how often interest is compounded and when is subject to each institution's rules. Passbook savings accounts are useful for transitory custodial and guardian funds if the sums are not substantial.

Safety and Risk

Passbook savings accounts are about as safe as the full faith and credit of the U.S. government if they are insured by the Federal Deposit Insurance Corporation (FDIC) and if they do not exceed $100,000. Since this government agency is backed by the federal government, there is virtually no likelihood that depositors will not be paid off in full should their individual bank or thrift fail. If the depository institution is insured only by a state agency, that fact alone is enough to wave a red flag. Depositors in Rhode Island recently saw the unhappy results when their accounts were insured solely by the state.

Transaction Costs

Banking institutions did not charge for opening and maintaining a passbook savings account before deregulation. Since deregulation a number of banks cease to pay even minimal passbook interest if the balance falls below a preset minimum, because they feel it is so costly to service small accounts. Some banks have even levied "negative" interest or service charges on small accounts in order to persuade the account holders to close them.

Liquidity and Maturity

Passbook savings accounts are immediately liquid provided the bank is open for business. However, such accounts are not easily negotiable since banks do not issue checks for such demand accounts. In order to pay someone else, a depositor must draw a money order or teller's check—an inferior way of doing business since it is difficult to halt payment if these are lost, and you are left with no receipt because the checks are not returned to the purchaser. Since a passbook savings account is a form of demand deposit, there is no maturity date: Interest is paid, in the better banks, from day of deposit to day of withdrawal, and on the average monthly balance.

Interest and Income

Passbook savings accounts pay the lowest rate of interest of all depository accounts. In order to overcome that rate differential, some banks offer a number of free services, such as free checking accounts and/or bank charge cards if the depositors will leave substantial funds in these accounts. The accounts will never yield more than their stated rate of interest, although different methods and times of compounding will somewhat alter their yield even when the rates are similar (see Appendix D). Today these accounts are perhaps the least worthwhile interest-bearing vehicles for saving money for college, whether in the long or short term.

NOW and Super-NOW Accounts

Definition

First started in New England by a savings bank, NOW accounts (Negotiable Order of Withdrawal) have spread throughout the United States. They enable a depositor to earn interest on a demand deposit, a checking account. Regular or personal checking accounts (along with business checking accounts) do not earn any interest. The NOW account presently earns interest at a rate of 2–3 percent, which is *less* than a passbook savings account.

The Super-NOW account is also a checking account that earns interest, but the rate is somewhat *less* than a money-market deposit account. It may have other names, such as liquid investment checking or super checking.

Safety and Risk

NOW and Super-NOW accounts receive the same FDIC protection as other bank deposits, up to $100,000 per account. One may keep more funds at one institution, but it would be wise to keep them in separate accounts, each with less than $100,000. For security, it is wise to insist on evidence that the bank is indeed a member of FDIC. It should never be assumed. State deposit insurance has shown to be second best.

Transaction Costs

There should be no charge for opening a NOW or Super-NOW account. The fees come later. Each bank has its own structure of fees if depositors do not keep a minimum balance (whether computed as a minimum, an average, or end-of-the-month or quarterly balance). For NOW accounts banks require anywhere from $500 to $2,500 as a minimum balance. Many offer free checking services in addition to the 2–3 percent interest if that balance is maintained. When the balance falls below the minimum, there is a monthly maintenance fee.

For Super-NOW accounts, the minimum balance is usually $2,500, though some banks have lowered it to $1,000. Since the rate of interest in a Super-NOW account is higher by one or two percentage points than a NOW account, a fall in the balance below the minimum will reduce the interest rate to the NOW level.

Liquidity and Maturity

NOW and Super-NOW accounts are quite liquid, enabling depositors to make third-party payments. There is no maturity date on this type of demand deposit and funds can be withdrawn at will. However, the minimum balance must be maintained in order to receive the best NOW or Super-NOW rate.

Interest and Income

Interest rates for NOW accounts are slightly lower than passbook accounts, about 1 or 2 percentage points lower. Consequently, there is not much incentive in keeping short- or long-term savings in these accounts. There are other alternatives for planned college savings that are equally safe. NOW and Super-NOW accounts perhaps have a place as repositories of transaction monies—funds destined to be paid out shortly after they are paid in. Thus, they may be useful as a custodian, guardian, or trust account as monies are moved into other instruments, or to pay imminent college bills. Indeed, these accounts are useful for college students since they can continue to earn some interest while they attend school and are obliged to pay bills. But in the final analysis, these accounts will only pay out the principal, plus accumulated interest, and no more. Rates in NOW and Super-NOW accounts do change: These accounts do not lock in a fixed interest rate.

Money-Market Deposit Accounts

Definition

One of the first results of financial deregulation was the authorization of depository institutions (commercial banks, savings and
loan associations, credit unions, mutual savings banks) to offer
money-market deposit accounts to compete with the money-
market funds of the mutual-fund management companies and
brokerage houses. Commencing on December 14, 1982, the
money-market deposit accounts became an alternative savings
vehicle. These accounts have their interest rates set by the banks
or thrifts, usually on a monthly basis. While the rates are a reflection of rates in the wholesale money markets, they are basically administered or set by the institution. This is in contradistinction to the money-market funds, which set rates based solely
on their dealings in the money markets (after allowing for a small
management fee).

Safety and Risk

Money-market deposit accounts are insured up to $100,000 by
the FDIC if the savings institution is covered by such protection.
This insurance thus eliminates the risk of individual institutional
bankruptcy. Money-market deposit accounts are considered safer
than money-market funds, which for the most part have no such
comparable protection. Thus it is possible to achieve close to the
highest prevailing money-market rates at your local savings institution since there is no limit to the highest rate under current
law. National advertising occasionally makes distant rates look
more attractive than local ones, but among the first questions to
be asked is what type of insurance will cover your account. Not
all institutions are obliged to have deposit insurance.

Transaction Costs

As a general rule, depository institutions do not charge a start-up
fee for a money-market deposit account. Nor are there any trans-

action costs if the account exceeds the minimum balance. Money-market deposit accounts initially required a $2,500 deposit to start, but accounts starting with $1,000 are now offered by many banks. There are, however, some limitations on the number of transactions that can be made monthly—only six to third parties, of which only three can be made by checks on the account. Some banks sharply penalize depositors who write more than three checks a month on a money-market deposit account.

Liquidity and Maturity

Money-market deposit accounts assure immediate liquidity, provided that the bank is open. However, some banks do not issue checks on these accounts so it is sometimes awkward to make payments from them. There are no maturity dates on money-market deposit accounts since they are basically a form of demand deposit.

Interest and Income

There is, of course, no chance for capital appreciation beyond the compounded interest that accrues to the account. These accounts will keep a depositor earning close to the best prevailing rate of interest at any given moment. However, they cannot and do not lock in a high yield as rates are subject to monthly changes, if not more frequently in some instances. Some banks have dual yields: Accounts with substantial assets, above $10,000 or $25,000, obtain a slightly better rate. Nevertheless, money-market deposit accounts are viewed by many depositors as the best demand account with the guarantee of safety of principal by the federal government. However, they are open to interest-rate risk, and there was a period in the mid-seventies when money-market funds paid no more than passbook accounts and, for a while, even less.

Initially, both money-market funds and the new money-market deposit accounts were viewed as places to park money temporarily while awaiting investment possibilities. Increasingly, they are viewed as an end in themselves, and as a surrogate for Treasury bills. Therefore, they are an excellent short-term demand account for college savings. They may not be the optimum long-term investment since they do not lock in a predictable yield, but they do provide optimum savings power if interest-rate trends are ambiguous.

CERTIFICATES OF DEPOSIT

Definition

Certificates of deposit (CDs) achieved notoriety as a way for banks to raise capital and for lenders to receive more return than was allowed by Federal Reserve regulations for small depositors. In the early sixties a market developed in this rather old financial instrument as banks started to trade negotiable CDs of $1 million and more. Banks started a retail business in CDs by offering them to small depositors in denominations from $100,000 all the way down to $500. Since these were not deposits, strictly speaking, but IOUs of the individual bank, they managed to skirt the regulations about higher yields until these regulations were first eased and later withdrawn.

The retail CDs of $100,000 or less are also insured by the federal government's FDIC, as are actual bank deposits. However, the small CDs (unlike their wholesale brothers) are not negotiable, as no secondary market exists for them.

Safety and Risk

Since CDs of $100,000 or less are insured by the FDIC of member depositories, investors in these bank securities need not have any doubt about their safety. However, not all banks and thrifts are so insured, which makes their debt paper risky. In shopping this market, savers must be especially careful since they may well find that the highest yields are not protected by such insurance. And it is these very banks or thrifts that have run into financial problems in the past since their costs for money were excessive.

Transaction Costs

There are no initial costs for a CD. But many savers have come to grief when they attempted to close out a CD before it reached its maturity date. Banks will penalize the holder by withholding 31 days of interest for a CD of one year or less. For longer maturities, the penalty is three months' interest, though individual institutions can increase that penalty. The penalty can be disproportionately stiff if the CD has to be cashed in early in its life.

Liquidity and Maturity

CDs are definitely not liquid instruments. In return for their higher yield compared to money-market deposit accounts, depositories insist upon penalties if the CDs are cashed in. There have been cases where some actually refused to pay out their CDs before maturity. However, brokerage houses are active in the CD market, brokering funds for their clients. Sometimes they maintain a secondary market in these nonnegotiable instruments, thus allowing a client to avoid a penalty if a CD must be cashed in before maturity.

Interest and Income

CDs are one of the best tools for families concerned with long-term college savings. CDs can be had in virtually any denomination, up to the $100,000 jumbo variety. They lock in a relatively high yield compared to savings plans. And they can be designed to mature in 6 to 60 months, or sometimes even longer. By judiciously timing their due dates, one can have CDs maturing sequentially, say annually as the tuition bills come due. CDs only return their original principal, plus compounded interest. The further away the maturity date, the higher the rate of interest (and yield) under the normal dictates of the yield curve. Thus the rate for a five-year CD is usually better than for a two-year CD. Should a family use CDs as their prime method to fund an education, ideally they should start five years before college commences and buy a new CD every year for the next four years to maximize interest payments. Many savings institutions will also work out a timetable: If you tell them how much you would like to have at a maturity date, they will tell you how much money you must initially deposit. In short, they offer designer CDs personally fitted for tuition plans.

MONEY-MARKET FUNDS

Definition

One of the most innovative savings plans in the last 20 years or so arose not from within the banking system but outside it. The development of money-market funds, a form of mutual fund, gave the small- and medium-size saver access to competitive or free money-market rates. Federal regulations dating back to the thirties set a ceiling on the interest rate savings institutions could offer to their depositors. As long as prevailing interest rates were low, depositors did not care about such ceilings. But in the face of growing inflation, they searched for mechanisms that circumvented arbitrary government regulations.

Money-market funds were established by investment management companies (later joined by brokerage houses) that took deposits from individuals, pooled them, and purchased the underlying assets of the money-market fund. Instead of common stock, they bought high-yielding debt instruments that traded in the money markets but were off-limits to small- and medium-size depositors since their minimum size was at least $10,000. They bought obligations of the U.S. government, CDs of banks, banker's acceptances, and commercial paper. These obligations are of relatively short duration, averaging about 30 days to maturity. Investors in money-market funds can buy any amount of shares, after an initial purchase of $1,000 or $2,500, and shares are denominated at $1 each. The net asset value of the shares remains constant at $1, and the accrued interest is issued as additional shares.

Safety and Risk

Unlike the comparable money-market deposit accounts, which were developed by the banks and thrifts to compete with them, money-market funds are not insured by any federal agency. A few do have private insurance, but the majority do not. (However, some funds invest only in U.S. government paper, which is tantamount to a government guarantee.) Though most funds do not have insurance, there have been no bankruptcies in any of the funds, and the likelihood of such an action is very slim. Still, some depositors feel that bank money-market deposit accounts are worth the fractional difference in yields that management companies and brokers offer over banks.

Transaction Costs

There are no transaction costs for money-market mutual funds. Depositors are offered free checking from the investment management companies, or can simply ask for a check drawn on their account if the fund is administered by a brokerage house. Nor is there any limit to the number of transactions that can take place, unlike the money-market deposit accounts, which do have monthly restrictions.

Liquidity and Maturity

Money-market funds are quite liquid, especially the ones that issue a book of checks. Most of the funds, however, insist on minimum deposits, which vary from fund to fund but are often $500. And the same is true for withdrawals: Most money-market funds insist that checks drawn on accounts be no less than $500. So while there is free checking, the money-market funds are not a replacement for a regular checking account. As with the bank money-market deposit accounts, there are no maturity dates for these demand accounts.

Interest and Income

While originally conceived as a temporary haven for funds while awaiting investment opportunities, it is now clear that money-market funds have become an end in themselves. They do not lock in an interest rate, but may fluctuate weekly. They are also useful for long-term holdings, but perhaps somewhat better yields are obtainable in other long-term investments. The funds are useful for the parents of college students, who may be obliged to meet unexpectedly large expenses throughout the college year, since they still earn income on their balances.

The question often arises as to whether the money-market deposit accounts offered by the banks or the money-market funds offered by the management companies and financial services companies provide the better return. While the banks initiated money-market deposit accounts with high teaser rates, funds today pay a slightly better rate—from 0.25 percent to 1.50 percent.

Finally, it should be noted that there are hundreds of money-market funds. Though most of the underlying assets are combinations of government paper, CDs, commercial paper, and banker's acceptances, there are some devoted to more specific purposes. As noted before, some funds invest only in government paper, some only in tax-free municipals, and still others in high-yielding corporate debt of less than investment grade quality. One must suit the fund to the intended purpose: For college planning it might be appropriate to be invested in a conservative fund, such as one that specializes in Treasury securities, and also in another that is likely to maximize return by investing in low-quality or "junk" bonds.

U.S. SAVINGS BONDS

Definition

Savings bonds, long considered a good patriotic investment but a dubious financial one, have been given a face lift in order to compete with other financial opportunities. Today they make an excellent vehicle for long-term college savings, especially for parents who cannot lay their hands on large sums. Indeed, they are particularly suited for parents who are obliged to save small sums periodically.

Today U.S. savings bonds come in two series, EE and HH. The EE are available in face value denominations of $50, $75, $100, $200, $500, $1,000, $5,000, and $10,000. The purchase price for any of these bonds is half the face value. Thus the interest is not paid out but accrues in redemption value, which is paid out when the bonds are cashed.

The HH bonds have face value denominations of $500, $1,000, $5,000, and $10,000. They cannot be bought new as an original issue, but must be received in exchange for outstanding series EE, E bonds, and Savings Notes (Freedom Shares), which must have redemption value of $500 or more.

Safety and Risk

U.S. savings bonds naturally have the full faith and credit pledge of the federal government. As such, these bonds have no credit risk. They do, however, have an interest-rate risk since very high rates of inflation would reduce the purchasing power of the redeemed bonds. In other words, the government guarantees that you will get your money back, but it does not guarantee that even with accumulated interest you might not lose some purchasing power. This was precisely the problem in the seventies when U.S. savings bonds fell into disrepute.

Transaction Costs

There are no transaction costs to purchase these government savings bonds, which can be bought at any depository institution, through a payroll savings plan, or through your employer. In fact, these registered bonds will be replaced free of charge in case of fire, theft, or loss.

Liquidity and Maturity

Savings bonds are not liquid investments. Indeed, they cannot be redeemed for the first six months. Series HH may be redeemed after six months from the date of issue, and then at any time of the owner's choosing. Unlike Series EE, interest is paid semiannually at a rate of 4 percent, reaching maturity 10 years after purchase. Neither series can be transferred, sold, or used as collateral for loans. The government limits the amount any one person can purchase to $30,000 face value each year.

Interest and Income

Series EE bonds have a floor of 4 percent per annum as of March 1, 1993, if they are held for at least five years, or receive interest at 85 percent of the average return during that time on marketable Treasury securities with five years remaining to their maturity, whichever is higher. Interest will be compounded semi-annually. If interest rates for Treasury notes are 10 percent, then bond owners will receive 8.5 percent instead of 4 percent.

Interest on Series HH bonds, the ones received upon exchange of EE or other savings bonds, is paid semi-annually at a straight 4 percent per annum. A $1,000 face value bondholder will receive two checks for $20 each year. This interest is taxable, but not by the state or local authorities. Series EE bonds are also taxable by the federal government, but the tax is deferred until the bonds are cashed in, disposed of, or reach maturity. Clearly, these bonds give great security and a reasonable rate of return to parents just starting a college savings plan. While they offer a good rate of return if general interest rates remain at or below 4 percent, they do have "opportunity costs" (lost income) if inflation heats up and interest rates again reach double digits as they did in the early 1980s. The opportunity costs are then 15 percent (the reciprocal of 85 percent) of the prevailing interest rates for comparably guaranteed government paper, such as Treasury bills or notes.

Finally, the government has recently enacted a bonus for parents saving for their children's education. Parents are now exempt from tax on interest income earned on Series EE savings bonds purchased after December 31, 1989, if the principal and interest from the bonds are used to pay college tuition.

There are some limitations: the taxpayer must be over age 24 when the bonds are purchased and must be the original purchaser of the bonds. For married couples filing jointly, the exemption is gradually phased out on adjusted gross incomes of between $60,000 and $90,000. For single taxpayers and heads of households the exemption phases out between $40,000 and $55,000. (These figures are adjusted annually for inflation.)

TREASURY BILLS, NOTES, AND BONDS

Definition

Government paper is considered the safest savings investment in the world, and the Treasury has always paid off holders of its obligations on time. In brief, there is no market or credit risk in the purchase of Treasury securities. There is, however, interest-rate risk, a risk inherent in any fixed-interest investment.

The Treasury has three kinds of debt obligations: bills, which are short term—90, 180, or 360 days (13, 26, or 52 weeks); notes, which are 1 to 10 years in duration; and bonds, which are 10 to 30 years. The bills are discounted from their face value, $10,000, and redeemed at maturity at full face value. How long they are held and how deep the discount determine the yield to the investor. Notes and bonds are interest bearing, paying interest semi-annually. The notes, in $1,000 or $5,000 denominations, are registered to the purchaser, but bonds, also in $1,000 denominations, may be had in bearer, registered, and book-entry form.

Safety and Risk

As mentioned, there is no credit risk with Treasury paper since it has the explicit pledge of the faith and credit of the federal government. Barring some cataclysmic event, you always will receive your principal plus the accrued or coupon interest. You may get back, however, less purchasing power rather than more. Anyone who bought 10-year Treasury notes in 1980 at the prevailing rate of 7.35 percent received back their $1,000 in 1990, plus $735 of interest (in addition to some further interest generated by the semi-annual income). However, periods of prolonged inflation play havoc with fixed-interest securities. If the 1990s are a period of deflation, this should be less of a concern.

Transaction Costs

There are no transaction costs when government paper is purchased directly from one of the 12 regional Federal Reserve

Banks. Nor is there any fee when the obligations mature and are cashed in. Three- and six-month bills are auctioned off each week, two-year notes once a month, and other note and bond refunding whenever the Treasury feels a need to go to market. In the case of the $10,000 Treasury bill, you pay full face value, but the government immediately returns the difference, in a sense pre-paying the interest rate as determined in the auction. If filling out the bidding forms is too much trouble, banks and brokers will purchase for you for a nominal commission. The secondary government market is massive, so it is possible to sell or buy Treasury securities before maturity dates, again for small commission fees.

Liquidity and Maturity

Since there is such a large secondary market in government securities, they can be turned into cash at a moment's notice. They are, in short, the most liquid of investments. With such a wide variety of maturity dates, from a few days to 30 years, it is possible to customize purchases to fit with college tuition needs.

Interest and Income

With the range of maturities available, it is important to understand the simple logic of the yield curve. It can be found represented in the business sections of daily newspapers. In normal circumstances, the further away the maturity of a fixed-interest security, the higher the interest rate, up to a certain point. After roughly 10 years, the curve becomes a plateau. The simplest explanation is that the more distant the maturity date, the less certain the lender is to get back his or her principal and interest, let alone equivalent purchasing power. The yield curve represents a tradeoff between relative certainty in the near term and uncertainty in the far term.

Beyond the interest rates represented by the yield curve, a saver's bills, notes, and bonds will be affected by current interest rates. Interest rates and fixed-rate securities move inversely to each other: When interest rates go up, the price of the securities goes down, and vice versa. If the purchased securities are held to maturity, the initial interest rate is also the yield to maturity. If the Treasury securities are bought in the secondary market, the yield is likely to be quite different from the coupon rate. A $1,000 bond with a 10-percent coupon will yield 11 percent when its price is $909, and it will yield only 9 percent when its price is $1,111.

Since fixed-rate instruments can fluctuate quite widely, it is possible to buy and sell Treasury securities for capital gains. This can be done without any penalty for premature sale, with just nominal commission fees. For parents with long-range savings plans, it is advisable to buy and put away these securities. Trading securities for capital gains is best left to professionals. But it is important to bear in mind that the price of fixed-interest securities such as Treasury notes and bonds does vary, sometimes quite dramatically. A premature or forced sale of these obligations may result in substantial loss. Therefore, it is important for parents to time their needs and correlate them with maturity dates. A certain flexibility is advisable: Do not have all securities reaching maturity at once. There may well be a need for additional monies for preparatory work or private secondary school before the child is ready for college.

Treasury notes and bonds have a coupon rate that dictates the semi-annual payments. If these obligations are sold at par or face value, the yield to maturity is explicit. Treasury bills, less important for long-term planning since their maximum maturity is only one year, have no coupon rate. They are sold at a discount from face value. The size of the discount indicates the yield. If you buy a one-year Treasury bill for $10,000 and the government immediately returns $1,000, then the yield is not the 10-percent discounted rate, but 11.11 percent since $1,000 is returned on $9,000.

GOVERNMENT AGENCY SECURITIES

Definition

Treasury bills, notes, and bonds are not the only federal obligations in the marketplace. There are other government agencies and government-guaranteed or -sponsored organizations of a quasi-official nature that issue debt instruments. Some of the more common ones are: Federal National Mortgage Association (FNMA); Bank for Co-ops; Federal Farm Credit; Student Loan

Marketing; Federal Home Loan Bank; World Bank; Inter-American Development Bank. The face value of these bonds starts at $1,000, but minimum investments may be as high as $25,000.

Unlike Treasury securities, these bonds are sold by syndicates of investment banking and brokerage houses that in turn retail them to private investors. In order to make it worthwhile for all concerned, they usually offer yields that are one half of 1 percent or 1 percent more attractive than Treasury securities of comparable maturity.

Safety and Risk

Some of these bonds are backed by the full faith and credit pledge of the U.S. government, while others have lesser guarantees. The lack of the explicit government pledge also contributes to the slightly higher yield of agency paper. It does appear that the government would be extremely reluctant to allow any of these agencies to face a liquidity crisis, much less default. In that sense, they have an implicit pledge though not a legal one. Many investors, therefore, have taken advantage of these higher yields without assuming any greater risk.

Transaction Costs

Since these issues are sold to the public by the financial community rather than the issuers, there is a small brokerage commission for issues already in the market. There is no sales charge if you buy them directly from the underwriters of the issue. Moreover, there is no penalty for selling these issues in the broad secondary markets before their maturity, only a sales commission.

Liquidity and Maturity

Agency issues are somewhat less liquid than Treasuries. This means that there is a larger spread between brokers' bid and ask prices. This is especially true if the investor is buying or selling just a few bonds. There is a wide range of maturity dates, from a few months to 20 or more years.

Interest and Income

The high yields and implied safety of federal agency paper make it eminently suited as a savings vehicle for the yield-conscious parent. The only drawback is that it is difficult to purchase small amounts of bonds without sacrificing some price concession. There are, though, some mutual funds that specialize in high-yielding government issues, which are appropriate for small savers. Interest rates follow the yield curve—the further away the maturity, the greater the yield. Yields on agency paper range from one half of 1 percent to 1 percent over Treasury securities under normal circumstances. After-tax yields may be changed by the tax status of individual issues. Some are free of state and local taxes, some not; but all are generally subject to federal taxes unless they are in a tax-free or tax-deferred account. If these bonds are sold before maturity, the usual rules for capital gains or losses apply.

MORTGAGE-BACKED SECURITIES

Definition

In recent years a new type of debt security was developed based on a pool of residential mortgages. The pool of mortgages is then divided into pieces and investors are sold a proportionate share of the interest payments on the mortgage as well as a portion of the principal. These mortgage-backed securities are known as pass-throughs since the public agencies and private companies that sponsor them are simply transferring interest and payment to the investors, usually on a monthly basis. There is no fixed life for mortgage-backed securities, nor is the yield precisely ascertainable since it depends on payback schedules and early mortgage termination. The government-sponsored and/or -owned companies that sell mortgage-backed securities are primarily the Government National Mortgage Association (Ginnie Mae), Federal Home Loan Mortgage Corporation (Freddie Mac), and Federal National Mortgage Association (Fannie Mae). Some private corporations also offer pass-through certificates.

Safety and Risk

Certificates issued by government-affiliated organizations are considered to be very safe since they are explicitly backed by the full faith and credit of the federal government or implicitly carry such a pledge. Private companies usually have insurance against mortgage borrower default. Therefore, pass-through certificates are reasonably sure of providing timely payments of interest and principal even though the exact sum may be undetermined.

Transaction Costs

New issues of certificates—usually in $25,000 slices and $5,000 increments—may be sold for a flat fee or at a slight markup. Either way, the charges are nominal. Since a $25,000 purchase is considerable and cuts out the smaller investor, mutual funds or unit trusts have started to offer fractional shares starting at $1,000.

Liquidity and Maturity

With the growing interest in mortgage-backed securities, a large secondary market has developed. It is therefore easy to sell certificates before they mature. But they are essentially investments to be held for the long term, usually a 12-year average life. Like all fixed-interest investments, the value of the certificate will fluctuate inversely to the prevailing interest rates. However, there are no interest penalties for selling before maturity.

Interest and Income

For parents saving for college tuition, the mortgage-backed securities offer some of the highest yields among federal guaranteed obligations, but their appeal is primarily to investors who wish not only higher yields but also monthly income. This latter point is not advantageous for the long-distance saver since part of each monthly payment contains repayment of principal as well as interest. Unless that income is put immediately back into some other interest-bearing account, there is the very real danger that the monies will be dissipated. Some brokers arrange that monthly income be deposited to money-market accounts when received. When that is done, it can actually be beneficial to the overall yield since reinvestment opportunity is monthly rather than semi-annually.

While not too many parents have the ability to invest in a new Ginnie Mae for $25,000, it is still possible to buy an older certificate whose principal has been paid down substantially. For example, a certificate with an 8 percent interest rate issued eight years ago has had 45 percent of the principal repaid, leaving $13,750 to be repaid. Should the current rate be higher, say 11 percent, the 8 percent certificate will sell at a discount, perhaps 85 percent, making the price to the investor $11,688 ($13,750 × 0.85). The problem with Ginnie Maes, as with other interest-bearing securities, is how to reinvest the interest income so that it yields as much as the original investment. This is particularly urgent for parents saving for college since mortgage-backed securities are throwing off income 12 times a year. While the high yields are desirable, the saver must correlate a way to employ the income and occasional windfall prepayments. Some investors have turned to mutual funds that automatically reinvest income in further Ginnie Maes.

ZERO-COUPON BONDS (TREASURIES)

Definition

Zero-coupon bonds have quickly achieved a preeminent position in long-term planning for families. They answer a number of critical issues for savers: They are virtually riskless; they offer relatively high yields compared to other interest-bearing securities; they can be accumulated for small sums. And perhaps most important for long-term savings for college, they lock in high yields.

A rather new financial instrument developed in the early eighties, zero-coupon bonds are deeply discounted bonds of the Treasury that do not pay semi-annual interest as do ordinary bonds. They produce earnings by rising to the face value ($1,000) over a series of years. This return of earnings is really compound interest on the initial invested sum. The principal of compounding makes for dramatic results. The Treasury has started to issue Separate Trading of Registered Interest and Principal of Securities (STRIPS), but many zero-coupon bonds are fabricated by investment banking houses. They take the basic Treasury securities and deposit them with a custodial bank, which separates the corpus and the interest coupons. The investment banker then issues certificates or receipts based on the underlying Treasury paper. These receipts go under different names depending on the investment banking house that issued them: Certificates of Accrual on Treasury Securities (CATS) and Treasury Investment Growth Receipts (TIGRS), among others.

Safety and Risk

Though the CATS and TIGRS certificates do not have the full faith and credit pledge of the government, as do the underlying Treasury securities, the custodial arrangement eliminates almost all of the risk. Even if the investment banking house that created or packaged the certificates runs into trouble, the receipts are likely to be as sound as the government paper that backs them.

Transaction Costs

It is possible to buy new zero issues without any commission costs, especially the STRIPS, in $1,000 multiples purchased from the Treasury. Brokers receive compensation from the underwriting investment house. Purchases in the secondary market are subject to a small markup or spread, as is the case should they be sold prematurely. CATS are listed among New York Stock Exchange bonds, but the other variations are sold in the over-the-counter market.

Liquidity and Maturity

Zero-coupon bonds are long-term investments, but a secondary market exists should it become necessary to terminate the holding before maturity. There is a wide range of government-backed zero-coupon bonds, maturing in anywhere from 1 or 2 years to

30 years. Most of them have call protection, that is, the government will not redeem the issues prematurely. One of the by-products of the lack of interest payments is that the zero-coupon bonds are volatile, rising when interest rates drop and falling when interest rates rise.

Interest and Income

Zero-coupon bonds defer paying any interest until they mature. Thus they lock in a yield for the life of the issue, compounding the interest on the interest. Ordinary bonds also lock in a fixed yield, but they have no mechanism to reinvest the semi-annual payments at comparable rates. This is especially important in building savings for college tuition. By investing small sums, starting with a child's birth, the magic of compound interest will produce a fund that may well be three, four, or five times the contributed monies. You will know ahead of time exactly what funds will be available on maturity. For example, a zero-coupon bond can be purchased for $520 which will mature in 2004—a yield of 6.21 percent compounded. By buying $10,000 face value for $5,200, parents will have nearly doubled their principal in a decade. If interest rates remain stable, a highly unlikely proposition, parents of a newborn child can presently triple their funds before the freshman year in these government-guaranteed bonds. To take advantage of fluctuating interest rates, it is perhaps best to buy a number of bonds each year rather than all at once. Under the tax code, taxes on imputed interest must be paid by the parents until the child is 14 years old. Zeros are also useful in individual retirement accounts or Keoghs since they are tax deferred.

ZERO-COUPON BONDS (MUNICIPALS AND CORPORATES)

Definition

A rising market has developed in zero tax-free municipals and corporate bonds. Municipals are tax-free issues of states, towns, counties, cities, colleges, and various authorities. Since they are free from all federal, state, and city taxes, they have somewhat lower yields than taxable bonds. These zeros are very similar to Treasury zero-coupon bonds discussed in the previous section. They are issued at a deep discount and do not pay semi-annual interest. When the bonds reach maturity, they are paid off at full face value. Zero municipals, called M-CATS or Municipal Receipts, received a major boost in popularity with the passage of the 1986 tax act. These can be accumulated in a child's name with no tax liability. Corporate zeros are a better bet for building a nest egg since their yields are higher than Treasuries or municipals. The corporate zeros are also issued at a deep discount with no semi-annual coupons.

Safety and Risk

To save interest costs, the federal government will not call in or redeem bond issues if prevailing interest rates are considerably lower. Municipalities and corporations are prone to calling their bonds, unless the bond indenture specifically prohibits it. If you are tempted by tax-free municipals and corporates, make sure they have a no-call provision. Zero municipals avoid this problem since the underwriters of these custodial receipts are making, in a sense, a mutual fund of these stripped instruments. Thus, they have removed the risk of an early call. In addition, some issues are collateralized with Treasury securities, giving them total security.

One problem with non-Treasury zeros is that while most decent-size municipalities are likely to be intact in 20 or 30 years, there is no guarantee that a small town or special issuing authority won't wither. There is even less certainty with a business, even a blue-chip business. In short, there is market risk, a feature virtually unknown in Treasury securities. In order to avoid this problem, there are funds of corporate zeros to diversify the risk implied by the higher yields.

Transaction Costs

When bought directly from the underwriters, there is no commission charge. However, in the secondary market there is a small brokerage charge to buy such securities. If the investor buys a mutual fund or unit trust there may be a sales charge, though some are sold on a no-load basis (that is, without a sales charge).

Liquidity and Maturity

An investor can select any of a range of maturity years to coordinate with tuition bills. The newer issues of M-CATS and Municipal Receipts have a series of short maturities—from 1 to 10 years. They are highly liquid but the price will fluctuate, which could be a disadvantage if they are sold before maturity. There is a distinct benefit with the municipals over Treasury or corporate zeros. No tax is due or imputed to the accrued interest. While they are tax free, they might impact on social security benefits if adjusted gross income is over $25,000 for a single parent or $32,000 for couples.

Interest and Income

If planned for sequential maturity, the bonds will come due as each school year commences. Therefore, it is worthwhile to ladder purchases. Since there is a large market of these bonds, it is possible to buy additional securities of your target maturities in subsequent years. This procedure may also even out the inevitable interest rate volatility.

MUNICIPAL BONDS

Definition

Municipal bonds, usually sold in $5,000 units, are obligations of towns, states, local authorities, colleges, and other entities that have a tax-free status. The federal government does not tax interest income from these bodies; nor do the state and local authorities tax their own issues, though they do tax each other's. Since municipals are tax free, they have traditionally sold at yields considerably below that of Treasury paper and far below yields of corporate paper. Of late, the yields have moved closer together.

All new municipals are now registered securities, but there are thousands of bearer issues in secondary markets.

Municipals generally have two sources of income: General obligation bonds draw their interest income from the taxing powers of local government; revenue bonds derive their income from fees, tolls, and charges of waterworks, terminals, airports, or turnpikes. Municipals are considered to be conservative investments with a default rate of less than 1 percent of all issues since the Great Depression. But default does happen occasionally.

Safety and Risk

For the most part municipals are quite safe, paying out their tax-free income twice yearly. Of late, bond issuers have started to insure their offerings through private insurance companies. This insurance usually results in credit services (Standard and Poor's, Moody's, and Duff and Phelps) assigning triple-A ratings. Conservative investors, so the traditional wisdom argues, should not invest in anything less than the first four quality ratings given by Standard and Poor's/Moody's: AAA/Aaa; AA/Aa; A/A; BBB/Baa—all the rest are speculative.

Transaction Costs

The minimum lot of municipals is $25,000 worth of bonds, but it is possible to buy occasional leftovers of a few bonds. If they are of large and well-known issues, there may not be too significant a concession in price, especially if they have to be sold before maturity. But selling unknown issues sometimes may only be done at distress prices. Dealers make their profits on the spread between bid and ask prices. Otherwise bond commissions are approximately $5 to $20 per bond, unless they are bought in the initial underwriting when there is no commission charge.

Liquidity and Maturity

If the bonds are going to be held to maturity, a sound practice if the parents obtained a good yield initially, liquidity is not an issue. But as noted, odd lots of relatively unknown bonds can usually be sold only at concession prices—down as much as 5 or 10 percent of their market price. Municipals often have call notices in their indentures, meaning that should interest rates go down, the municipality will attempt to save money by calling or retiring the expensive bonds and replacing them with a cheaper or lower coupon series. Call provisions can be avoided or their effect much reduced by buying shares of a closed-end unit trust or an open-end mutual fund. Such vehicles also eliminate the problem of selling prematurely at distress prices. But such funds may or may not have a load or commission charge, and they often yield one half of 1 percent or 1 full percent less than individual bonds.

Interest and Income

For high-income parents who wish to maintain control and ownership over their educational savings, municipal bonds are certainly sound holdings. The disadvantages are that their tax-advantaged yields are somewhat low, that they present the recurrent problem of reinvesting the interest income, and that they may be taxed through the back door. Since 1985 the government has required that if municipal bond interest, adjusted gross income, and half of a beneficiary's social security payments exceed $25,000 for singles or $32,000 for couples, then half the retiree's benefits may be taxed. While this provision is more likely to apply to grandparents than parents, it should be considered in establishing a college savings plan.

In order to compare taxable yields with nontaxable ones, divide the tax-free yield by 100 percent, minus the applicable tax bracket:

$$\frac{6\% \text{ (tax-free municipal)}}{100\% - 28\% \text{ (tax bracket)}} = 8.33\% \text{ (taxable yield)}$$

Someone in the 28 percent tax bracket would have to have an 8.33 percent taxable yield to have the same after-tax income as a tax-free municipal yielding 6 percent.

In order to combat inflation, the enemy of long-term, fixed-interest securities, a number of variations have appeared to improve yield and/or liquidity. Floating-rate issues adjust their yields periodically by way of complicated formulas. The result is a better yield and bonds that will fluctuate somewhat less as interest rates change. "Put" bonds give the owner the option of selling the bonds back to the issuer at prices fixed in advance in case interest rates rise. Both the floating-rate and put bonds give a long-term investor some needed protection against rising prices.

CORPORATE BONDS

Definition

Corporate bonds are sold in $1,000 denominations with fixed-interest coupons, even though some are sold in registered form as well as bearer form. Debentures are perhaps the most common form of bond, sold basically on the company's name and its ability and will to repay the borrowed funds sometime in the future. Mortgage bonds are somewhat more secure since they have specific assets pledged to pay them off. There are a number of variations in the bond world and a wide range of quality. Analyzing bonds is best left to professionals since a bond is essentially a promise to repay over a long period of time. Whether that promise is worth much remains the domain of the rating services. Standard and Poor's and Moody's rank bonds: The first four categories are investment grade, while anything below them is speculative. Bonds are attractive to conservative investors primarily because of their safety and their high yield. Corporate bonds often return 2 or 3 percent more than comparable Treasury securities.

Of late, a great deal of attention has focused on junk bonds, which very often are created as vehicles for mergers and acquisitions, and leveraged buyouts. These bonds are usually ranked by the rating services as speculative, rated Ba by Moody's or BB by Standard and Poor's, or worse. They have a dubious ability to pay bondholders their interest, and the coupon rates are extraordinarily high. Conventional wisdom argues against using junk bonds to finance a college education. However, some academic studies indicate that on balance they are not much riskier than more conservative bond holdings.

Safety and Risk

Bonds are far safer instruments than common stock, which depends on a company's earnings. Companies establish sinking funds to pay off the interest and principal due their bondholders. The quality of the "cover," the ability to pay off the bonds, is one of the key ingredients that the rating services use to measure the quality of bonds.

Transaction Costs

Costs for trading bonds are quite nominal: There are no charges for a new issue if it is bought from the underwriters and only about $5 per bond in the secondary market. There may be some price concession if the bond is infrequently traded or is little known. Consequently, it is best to buy debt issues of large corporations.

Liquidity and Maturity

Bonds are easily sold, whether listed on the New York Stock Exchange or traded in the over-the-counter market. Good quality bonds make an excellent vehicle for accumulating college funds, especially if they are in the name of the child, since they usually offer returns that are considerably higher than money-market deposit accounts or Treasury paper. But since bonds are promises over time, it is wise to purchase bonds only of solid corporations. There is such a variety of bond issues that it is not difficult to find maturity dates that coincide with college needs.

Interest and Income

Bonds, of course, have no inherent growth potential—the corporation promises only to pay back what you originally lent, plus accrued interest. Thus, it is solely the interest that is accumulated for savings, and that must be reinvested after it is paid out semi-annually. If one has found an issue with an advantageous yield, check to see if the bond offers call protection so that it will not be prematurely paid off. A 10 percent coupon may indeed be an excellent return, but if interest rates move sharply lower, it will motivate the company to call the bond and refinance its debt.

Bond prices move inversely with the prevailing rate of interest. Thus it is possible for bonds to move to a premium or a

discount from the original purchase price. This is one of the weak-
nesses of the bonds in a high-inflationary environment. However,
trading bonds for capital gains or losses is best left to professionals.
For college savers, intermediate-term bonds with maturity dates
ranging between 7 and 10 years will offer close to the highest
returns for fixed-interest securities.

COMMON STOCKS

Definition

Buying shares in corporations is one way that parents may dramatically increase their monies. Unlike all previously discussed
types of savings, common stocks do not rely solely on the return
of interest. It is possible to obtain profit from a gain in the ultimate
price of the securities, and it is possible to have additional dividend
income as well. Thus, equity ownership is a powerful tool for
parents preparing for college bills.

Shares are fractional ownership of businesses ranging from
the largest in America to the smallest venture-capital idea. The
stocks of over 40,000 American corporations, plus thousands of
foreign ones, are continuously traded in the secondary markets—
the New York Stock Exchange, the American Stock Exchange,
regional exchanges, and the over-the-counter market. Share
prices range from a few cents to hundreds of dollars, and the
quality of common stocks is as varied as their prices. Some common stocks, such as utilities and older established corporations,
pay healthy dividends while others, such as high-tech or new
business ventures, pay none.

Safety and Risk

Fixed-interest investments have only interest-rate risk, that is,
one may miss out on "opportunity costs," the higher rates that
may develop in competitive accounts or instruments due to inflation. In most of the depository accounts and fixed-interest securities there is no (or very little) credit or company risk. Savers and
investors will get back their original principal, plus the interest
due them. In common stock there is no such guarantee—there is

substantial company risk. Consequently, while there may be a place for equities in a college savings program, there should also be other savings and investments that are not subject to the vagaries of the marketplace. Some of the risk of equities can be reduced by diversifying a portfolio both as to time and as to industries. This can be done by averaging—that is, buying shares over periods of time—and buying shares in diversified industries such as manufacturing, service, high technology, agriculture, oil, and other sectors.

Transaction Costs

Buying and selling stock is not inexpensive, about 1 percent of the principal, depending on whether it is a discount or full-service brokerage house. It is possible to obtain shares without commission costs if the shares are part of an initial public offering or secondary offering. And some companies have dividend reinvestment plans to accumulate more shares without commission costs. However, all trades on the exchanges will be charged a commission when the broker acts as an agent. In the over-the-counter market, the broker is often acting as a dealer, making his profit not on a commission but on the spread between the bid (offer price) and ask (demand price).

Liquidity and Maturity

There are ready markets for most of the shares that are publicly traded. These continuous markets give shares the utmost liquidity with little price fluctuation between trades. Small investors can exit the market without concession pricing far easier than institutions can. Since common stock has no maturity date, shares are sold at the option of the owner.

Interest and Income

Common stocks can be profitable in two distinct ways: They can pay a dividend from the earnings of the corporation; and they can appreciate in price in the marketplace due to a positive outlook for the company. Unlike most other instruments discussed in this section, a portfolio of common stocks (or mutual funds) can exhibit a rate of return far in excess of most savings vehicles.

There is, however, a cautionary note to bear in mind. Shareholders of public corporations receive dividends only after all debts have been paid and the operating needs of the company have been met. Businesses raise, lower, and sometimes eliminate dividends without warning, depending solely on business conditions. In brief, dividend income can be unpredictable.

While capital appreciation is much to be desired, there is no guarantee that share prices will advance. Depending on the overall business cycle, the fortunes of the company, the state of the stock market, and a number of other conditions, your shares may or may not appreciate.

Common stocks are generally divided into three categories: blue chip stocks of leading corporations that pay stable dividends; growth stocks that pay some dividend income but have stronger appreciation potential; and speculative stocks that pay no dividends (since all earnings are put back into the business) but have the greatest growth potential.

A diversified portfolio should have some stocks from each category. For balance and safety, only a portion of your total college cost investment should be placed in common stocks.

INSURANCE

Definition

Parents of college-bound students must think of the unthinkable: the possibility of dying before sufficient funds have been accumulated for their children's education. Life insurance can protect one's heirs or other people for whom one is responsible in that eventuality. (Annuities, on the other hand, protect individuals from outliving their savings.) Traditionally, insurance companies sell ordinary life insurance, sometimes referred to as whole life or straight life. This policy is funded by premiums paid usually by the policyholder: Part of the premium goes into a reserve or cash-value account, which acts as a form of savings. This account may pay dividends or provide an option to purchase more coverage. The policyholder can borrow against this account, sometimes at relatively low rates of interest. The only way to collect the principal is, of course, to die. Under older policies it may still be possible to borrow funds at low rates for college costs. One is essentially borrowing one's own money. The incremental value or return on the cash value in most companies is something less than current money-market rates. In short, as a vehicle for building savings, insurance ranks rather poorly.

Many individuals, consequently, shy away from whole life and buy term insurance, which has no surrender or cash value. They then invest what would have been the additional premium costs in some other form of savings. In order to combat the erosion of inflation on insurance proceeds and savings, and to provide a better return on a policy's cash value, insurance companies have come up with a number of variations on the theme of life insurance. Adjustable-rate policies allow for increases and decreases in the premium or shortening or lengthening the premium payment period, and raising or lowering the benefits. Under universal life it is possible to have a higher level of benefits during a particular period. Premiums can also be adjusted within a wide range of parameters. Variable-rate policies accumulate cash value faster and allow for its accumulation in money-market-like funds, or equity funds. Thus there is a potential for a greater return from the cash value. Some policies tie the face value benefit to the portfolio of investments the policyholder has designated, but it maintains a minimum face value regardless of how poorly the investments perform. This variable rate is perhaps the best of the lot for someone attempting to accumulate funds within a life insurance format.

The loss of a number of deductible items, such as contributions to an IRA, under the 1986 tax law has made saving through life insurance policies increasingly popular. Single-premium life insurance can be bought with one lump-sum payment. Most of the premium goes into an investment pool where it accumulates on a tax-deferred basis. Later on the funds may be borrowed: The proceeds of the loan are not taxable.

Safety and Risk

There are 2,000 domestic insurance companies, but not all are equally reliable. It is even more difficult to analyze insurance companies than the policies they underwrite. However, *Best's Review* is a rating service that does rate them. Insurance companies are overseen by each state's insurance commission, so you can check with that office in case you have any doubt as to a company's record and its ability to honor claims promptly.

Transaction Costs

Insurance policies vary greatly both in policies and premiums. From the point of view of accumulating funds, insurance policies are a kind of forced savings. It is better than nothing, but far from an optimal way to save money. But of course that is not their primary purpose. Still, the cash-surrender value may provide an unrealized source of funds.

Liquidity and Maturity

Borrowing against an insurance policy is as American as apple pie. But an insurance policy is hardly a liquid investment. Whereas loan rates were low at one time, today most companies charge near-market levels of interest to policyholders. Unfortunately, the only way of cashing in on a policy is through death.

Interest and Income

Variable-rate policies are the only ones that provide a way to accumulate additional capital through mutual funds or other investment instruments. Monies earned in cash-value or reserve accounts are tax-advantaged, that is, they accumulate without any immediate tax liability. Single-premium life insurance may be a source of college funds. Since the policy must be funded by a large premium payment, there is immediate cash to be borrowed for college costs. Should the policyholder die before the loan is repaid, the beneficiary will receive the death benefit, less the outstanding loan. Finally, it is possible to buy a single-premium, dividend-paying policy issued by mutual life insurance companies. Funds distributed to policyholders, whether for living or college costs, are tax free as long as the monies taken out do not exceed the original premium. Insurance may never provide the best return on cash, but it does provide peace of mind. Finally, insurance proceeds are passed on tax free to heirs.

4

GIFTS

THE ROLE OF GIFTS

Generally, there are three legitimate ways to accumulate money: Work for it, borrow it, or receive it as a gift. In preparing to pay for college, the role of gifts is quite central, though parents, grandparents, relatives, and friends often neglect the subject. Certainly paying for a student's tuition and college costs is a major and direct form of a gift. This of course is a common, if little thought about, practice. However, a gift is a shift of capital that can have financial, legal, and tax considerations of major importance to both the donor and the recipient. When properly executed, a gift of money can have significant impact on lowering income taxes and even estate taxes. Most important, when properly executed, it can generate income to help pay for college.

Under the current tax code, a gift is *not* income. Thus, a gift has no bearing on the income of the donor (parent, grandparent, relative, or friend) and no tax consequence for the recipient. Or to put it the other way, a gift does not lower the taxable income of the donor or raise the taxable income of the donee. A gift is tax neutral for income tax purposes—a newborn or a graduating high school student is not a charity—and thus is not a tax-deductible expense.

While a gift generally does not have income tax consequences, there is a separate gift tax. It is of chief concern to the affluent since in recent years it has been liberalized. Donors can give up to $10,000 a year to any individual—child, stepchild, distant relative, or friend. (You may even give $10,000 a year to a complete stranger, though that does tax credulity.) A husband and wife can give up to $20,000 to a single individual. Any amount in excess of $10,000 to one individual is subject to the gift tax paid by the grantor. However, it is possible to give 10 gifts of $10,000 each without being subject to the gift tax. (There are two exceptions to the $10,000 limitation: One may give any amount to a dependent for medical expenses or to a student for tuition payments.)

The annual exclusion of $10,000 means that anything over that sum is subject to a tax. A $12,000 gift, less the $10,000 exclusion, would leave $2,000 subject to tax. In this case, the tax would amount to $360. A $50,000 gift would, after the $10,000 exclusion, leave $40,000 subject to the tax and a tax bill of $7,200. The tax starts at 18 percent with a maximum rate of 55 percent (see Appendix B).

However, no gift tax is likely to be paid, within limitations. A major tax reform act in the early eighties has allowed a unified credit to every American of $192,800. The gift tax, whether $360 or $7,200 in the above examples, would not be paid but applied against the credit. Unless the tax exceeded the credit, the tax would be considered paid in full. In short, the value of an equivalent gift would have to exceed $600,000 to use up the credit. (Presumably anyone with the wherewithal for these substantial gifts would not be overly concerned about planning for college costs.) Should you exceed the credit, then the tax must be paid the following year. If the credit is not exceeded, the balance of it may be applied against federal estate taxes.

INHERITANCES

The 1986 Tax Reform Act had virtually no effect on inheritance taxes—they remain the same as before. There has been no increase in the basic gift tax rates, but the undistributed income of estates and (nongrantor) trusts is now taxed at two brackets: The first $5,000 of taxable income is taxed at 15 percent; any excess is taxed at 28 percent. That may change some day, but most taxpayers feel strongly about being able to pass on wealth to their family and descendants. There have been attempts to increase capital gains taxes on either the transfer of inherited property or its sale. Congress has defeated these attempts, underscoring Senator Harry Byrd's observation that "death is not a loophole."

Inherited property (after estate taxes are paid) is basically not subject to levies on its appreciation. If shares were bought at $10 per share, but have a market price of $50 per share at the time of death, there is no tax on that appreciation. When the heirs sell the shares, they will measure their gain from the new basis of $50 per share at the time of death. If they do not sell the shares, it is possible for the shares to pass without tax to the next generation. The income produced by such assets is now taxed somewhat differently due to the reform act, but the assets are not taxed. That income, after taxes, can be used to pay for college expenses without invading the principal.

It bears repeating that the gift is *not* a deductible item against the donor's income tax, nor is it considered as income to the recipient. Gifts are made with after-tax income. And even gifts in excess of the $10,000 per year per recipient do not face an immediate gift tax unless they exceed the unified credit.

A gift—whether cash, securities, real estate, or an interest in a business—does have income tax implications for the donor. The money with which the gift property was originally bought was after-tax money, whether those funds came from earned income or capital. However, the purchase of the property or interest establishes a new tax basis both in time and in money.

It is this basis in time and money that will be used by the recipient of the gift should he or she decide to sell it. This is of significant tax value to a family since it shifts potentially high capital-gains income from appreciated property to a low tax bracket. So while the donee will pay *no* income or gift tax upon receiving the property, there will be an income consideration when the property or interest is sold. Needless to say, a cash gift would have no tax consequences as the funds are spent, but the recipient is taxed on the earnings of those funds for income tax purposes.

EXAMPLES OF GIFTS

To illustrate: A gift of (appreciated) property that had been in the family for years could be sold immediately after it was given to the recipient. The holding period for the property is no longer of any consequence under the 1986 tax act since there now is no distinction between long- and short-term ownership. The making of a gift thus changes the party responsible for the income tax, but it uses the acquisition date of the original purchase as the basis. When the recipient of the gift sells it, the tax basis is not the valuation on the day of the transfer, but on the original purchase date.

Some examples will show the income tax and gift tax implication of gifts:

- Grandparents jointly give their $100,000 homestead to their grandson. It was originally bought 20 years ago for $50,000. The grandson in turn sells his new gift to pay for and/or earn income for college. The grandparents have a gift tax obligation on the valuation ($100,000) of the homestead on the date of the transfer. Their gift tax is based on $100,000 less the $20,000 joint exclusion, or $80,000. The tax is $18,200. This tax can be applied against the unified credit and will not have to be paid unless it exceeds that credit.

- Parents give each 15-year-old twin 100 shares of General Widget, at present worth $70 per share. The original price of each share was $35 when purchased five years earlier. The parents suspect that the industrial economy may be in for a period of stagnation and weaker profits. They naturally have a number of options: (1) They could sit with the shares and defer any tax while receiving a dividend and hope for better times; (2) They could sell the shares and pay a tax on the $35 per share profit; (3) They could give the appreciated securities to their twins and divest themselves of the shares and the tax liabilities of the shares.

What are the tax and financial consequences of these three options? (1) By retaining the shares there will be no tax to pay until the shares are sold. The dividend income will continue, but there is no telling whether or not it might be cut. And the dividends will be taxed as ordinary income. The shares may fall to their original purchase price, thus wiping out any chance for capital gains. (2) The parents sell the shares for a capital gain of $7,000 to be taxed as ordinary income. (3) By passing on the shares as a gift, the parents have no income tax liabilities, whether the shares are sold or not. Nor is there a gift tax since it does not exceed $10,000 per child. If the shares are sold the day after they are received, the shares are still taxed as capital-gains income.

- An older, successful sister has made a quick killing in the real estate market. Land she purchased on January 1 for $10,000 rose dramatically to $50,000 by June 1. It may surrender much of that value if it is held too long. If the older sister sells it, she is faced with a substantial capital gain of $40,000. This will be taxed at her ordinary or full-tax rates. Since she earns over $100,000, she is in the 31 percent tax bracket. She stands to lose over $12,000 of her profits to taxes.

By giving the property to her younger, college-attending sister, the real estate operator has incurred a gift tax of $8,200. However, the tax does not exceed her unified credit, so there is no actual payment. The younger sister now has the choice of selling or keeping the property. Upon advice from her sister, she sells the property for $50,000. Her tax basis is $10,000. She has no other income, so the $40,000 gain is taxed as ordinary income (less her exemption and deduction)—nearly $6,000 of tax. The gift saved almost $5,000 in taxes.

Some Warnings

All the above examples illustrate that a properly timed gift can save the donor substantial income taxes without necessarily being subjected to a gift tax. The transfer can then provide income to the child or student, which will be taxed at a lower tax base than the donor. That, in essence, is the idea of income shifting.

There are some misconceptions about gifts that should be clarified. The actual amount of the gift is its true market value or fair value at the time the gift is made. It is of no consequence that the donors of the gift paid considerably less (or considerably more). As far as the gift tax is concerned, it is based on the fair value on the day of the transfer. Remember, this is in contradistinction to the recipient's tax basis, which is identical in time and dollar value to when the donor acquired the property originally.

A gift must have no strings attached. It is not in consideration for goods and services; it is not a loan to be later recaptured by the donor. Nor can it masquerade as a sale. Sales for some nominal sum cannot be treated as true sales since they are really gifts and subject to a gift tax. True value, for tax purposes, is an arm's length transaction: It is the price willing buyers and sellers arrive at without being under any obligation to buy or sell.

Sales that are tainted or manipulated by charging too much or too little, especially to family members, are likely to be challenged and taxed accordingly. A below-market sale or bargain sale is likely to create a capital gains tax for the donor and possibly a gift tax as well.

A gift must indeed be truly that. The donor must transfer and convey the actual cash, or property, or the right to the deed, title, bank account, or securities certificates. A gift is for present enjoyment, that is, the recipient (or his or her guardian, custodian, or trust) has total control of the gift and any income arising from the gift. If there are any reservations or any allowance for future interest in the property by the donor, the "gift" is not a true gift and thus reverts to taxable property of the donor.

A true gift may present certain problems for some parents or grandparents. While the tax advantage may be overwhelmingly clear and positive, they may, frankly, not trust their children's judgment. After all, once a gift is made, it is possible that the gift will be used (or misused) for frivolous or fanciful objects, such as stereo equipment, automobiles, and trips to Florida. Parents and other donors are left only with the force of moral persuasion. Though the gift was solely for educational purposes, the student may develop other ideas. In brief, a young person may not be ready to accept the responsibilities of substantial funds. In order to avoid that problem, parents and other donors may use other techniques to ensure that given funds are used to help pay for college and educational expenses.

THE UNIFORM GIFTS TO MINORS ACT

For a number of reasons, gifts may make financial sense from the point of view of taxes but be impractical for minors. Understandably, many minors have neither the knowledge nor the capacity to make judgments on substantial assets. Indeed, it may be virtually impossible for a minor to manage money since he or she has no legal standing for executing contracts in most states. This does not mean that minors cannot own property. At one time gifts to minors were executed through trusts, which entailed the formalities of a court and a guardian. In small matters this was not worthwhile, though trusts are still used and are especially useful for larger gifts. What developed and spread throughout the United States was a law that made it easy and cheap to pass on property to minors. A Uniform Gifts to Minors Act (UGMA) has been passed in every state; they are all rather similar. They provide a simple mechanism for passing on a gift to a minor without elaborate and expensive legal work. The gift is given to a custodian to administer on behalf of the minor. Custodians are most often parents or other adults within the immediate family—sometimes the donors, sometimes not.

Custodians should be knowledgeable about and attentive to the asset gift they are managing since they may be held legally responsible for its prudent administration. Prudence is the hallmark of guardians (and trustees), and the concept dates back to a landmark case in the early nineteenth century when Justice Samuel Putnam ruled:

> All that can be required of a trustee to invest is that he shall conduct himself faithfully and exercise a sound discretion. He is to observe how men of prudence, discretion, and intelligence manage their own affairs, not in regard to speculation but in regard to the permanent disposition of their funds, considering the probable income as well as the probable safety of the capital to be invested.

This became known as the Prudent Man Rule. What evolved over the years were various legal lists that defined and identified what were prudent investments. In general, the lists or categories tend to be rather conservative, erring perhaps on the side of safety and income instead of growth. Ultra-conservative guardians will make investments only from the legal list. While the prescriptions differ from state to state, in general they are: obligations of the United States; bonds of federal agencies, such as debts of Federal Land Bank, Federal Home Loan Bank, Federal National Mortgage Association, etc.; obligations of the state, city, county, or town; obligations of other states; bonds of the International Bank for

Reconstruction and Development (World Bank) or of the Inter-American Development Bank; bonds of Canada, or its provinces; bonds and/or debentures of corporations; and common stock of corporations that are listed on national stock exchanges. Custodians, however, are not mandated to use the list, but they are obliged to be cautious and responsible in investing the principal.

Almost any asset can be transferred as a gift (though restrictions differ slightly from state to state), but the most common are cash, stocks, bonds, mutual funds, life insurance policies, and, in some states, real estate. Custodians may convert property—they can sell the telephone stock and buy zero-coupon bonds or use the funds to buy United States savings bonds or Treasury bills—but they should never commingle the gift funds with their own no matter how closely related. Commingling of funds not only opens up a Pandora's box of conflicts, but probably will undermine the gift status for tax purposes. It may even be the cause of unnecessary litigation in the future. A new bank account or brokerage account should be opened for each minor and designated as a UGMA account with the name of the *minor* and the name of the *custodian*.

If the minor's name is absent, a true gift has not been made. The spouse of the donor is frequently named custodian since gifts under the UGMA are usually too small to hire a professional investment counselor, financial planner, or trust company. By and large, there is no penalty for poor judgment—the best investment vehicles can and sometimes do turn sour for a period of time. What is actionable and what may be held against the custodian is fraud, negligence, conflict of interest, and any indication of a lack of prudence. While few custodians are ever asked to account for their actions, since a child is not likely to ask for a reporting, there may be occasions when the custodian is forced to do so. Consequently, good record keeping is an important part of reducing a custodian's liability.

Since most gifts under the UGMA are relatively small, custodians are somewhat limited in their investment horizons. Bank accounts, money-market funds, or government bonds are the usual recipients of UGMA funds. In short, interest-bearing accounts or high-grade investment paper with a fixed yield are the most common use of these monies.

The interest and the principal of a UGMA account can be invaded, that is, used for the minor before that child reaches his or her majority. In general, the UGMA calls for the funds to be used for the minor's support, maintenance, and education. There is one major reservation, however: The funds should not be a substitute for parental obligations. If they are so used, they may be considered self-serving by the Internal Revenue Service. Should that be the case, then the gift's tax status is denied, and the account's income will be taxed to the parents. This is an important point to consider since such a result would destroy the concept of income shifting.

The investment income above $1,000 from a UGMA account is now taxed to the parent until the minor reaches the age of 14. This makes the tax benefit somewhat less attractive than under the old tax law if there is taxable income in the account. However, the UGMA should still be considered because it does create a separate pool of funds to be administered by parents. Income after the minor is 14 does receive preferential treatment since it is then taxed at the minor's rate rather than that of the parents. This guarantees three or four years of no taxation or low tax rates before college, depending on the amount of earned income. Before the minor is 14 years old, parents should consider four options for UGMA and other custodial accounts:

- United States savings bonds

- An insurance policy that provides tax-deferred growth

- Tax-exempt municipals

- Common stock or mutual funds that stress appreciation, not income

Any of these strategies (more fully discussed in the next chapter, "Taxes and Income Shifting"), or a combination of them, will ensure a lower tax bill but, more importantly, will provide capital growth. The emphasis in custodial accounts is high growth and low income before age 14, but growth *and* income after 14.

Gifts and custodial accounts serve another purpose as well: Complications from probate are partially avoided, and estate tax liabilities are reduced by giving away some of one's assets.

There are some drawbacks to the UGMA. Parents lose control of the funds perhaps earlier than they anticipated and perhaps before the child is ready to receive such a substantial gift. Under the UGMA, the account must be terminated and all funds turned over at the child's maturity. This age of maturity under the UGMA differs from state to state, but it is most often 18, 19, or 21 years of age; in a few states, such as New York, New Jersey, Maryland, and Delaware (where majority is 18), donors can ask for continued custodianship until 21. Once the funds are turned over, the child is free to do with them what he or she will; there is no obligation to use them only for education.

BORROWBACK REVISITED

Under the old tax code, it was possible for parents to use some creative solutions for college funding. One of the more popular ones was to borrow funds within the family. Under the 1986 tax code it may still be possible, but the benefits of borrowing are severely reduced. Formerly, parents and interested donors would give a gift of cash to the child and then borrow the funds back at a stated rate of interest. The child's age was irrelevant; what was important was that the gift had no strings attached and that the borrowed monies be secured by a formal promissory note.

The advantage of this borrowback arrangement was that the interest paid on the debt by the parents to the child was an expense that could be deducted from their income. On the other side, the child showed the interest payment as income. A high rate of interest was obviously preferable, but it had to be in line with some key benchmark such as the Treasury bond rate or the prime rate. If the rate was too high, the arrangement might look like a gift, and if too low, it might appear that the child's custodian or trust was not looking out for his or her best interests. Parents were thus able to take a significant interest deduction against their personal income, while the child had a source of income that either went untaxed or was taxed at a relatively low rate.

Parenthetically, for many years another legitimate ploy was lending children money and charging *no* interest. The funds were invested in the children's names so that interest, dividends, and capital gains would be taxable to them at their lower income tax rates. In 1984 the government limited the amount of a free loan to $10,000. Any sum above that had an imputed rate of interest added to the lender's taxable income, even if no interest was received.

The 1986 Tax Reform Act severely reduced the use of both borrowback arrangements and interest-free loans. Two provisions of the code work against those interest-shifting techniques. First of all, no interest deductions are allowed for consumer loans on credit cards, autos, or student loans.

Second, the provision of taxing parents for unearned or investment income above $1,000 from gifts given to their children who are under 14 years old sharply reduces the use of borrowback arrangements. Whether those gifts of cash or securities are in a UGMA or a trust account, the income from such assets will be taxed to the child at the parent's rate. Moreover, this is true even if the assets were given by grandparents or other relatives—the law states "regardless of the source of the assets creating the child's net unearned income."

5

TAXES AND
INCOME
SHIFTING

Every year the federal government diddles with the tax code in the pursuit of increased revenues, but also to address perceived inequalities or to implement social goals. The constant changes make long-term planning difficult. Nevertheless, buried within the 80,000-plus pages of revenue instructions are some nuggets along with the hard nuts. In short, there is good news and bad news in the latest edition of revenue enhancement, known as the Revenue Reconciliation Act of 1993.

However, it is first necessary to revisit an earlier tax act, the 1986 Tax Reform Act, in order to appreciate the direction of tax policies and their implications for parents, children, savers, investors, and the colleges.

The 1986 Tax Reform Act took aim at a variety of techniques that were used legitimately to shift income, as well as to avoid taxation through the use of shelters. For the most part, Congress hit the target. But hitting the target was not painless or without cost. The income tax system was progressive—the higher the income, the greater the percentage of income paid in taxes. Under the old system there were 14 different tax brackets, starting at 11 percent and ending at 50 percent. The basic income-shifting technique was to remove assets (and consequently the income or return from those assets) from the highest marginal tax brackets and place them in the lowest available tax brackets. Putting assets in the zero tax bracket, for instance in the name of a child, was best because exemptions and deductions virtually eliminated the first few thousand dollars of income from any serious taxation. Clearly, it was better to have income taxed at 0 or 11 percent than at 30 or 50 percent.

The 1986 act established three levels of personal taxation: 15, 28, and 31 percent. (In 1993, two additional brackets were added, 36 percent and 39.6 percent; see Appendix A.) The rates or tax brackets were lower than before, but there was little or no tax relief since many deductions were no longer allowed. One of the most significant ones was the loss of a personal exemption for a child—it now may be taken only once. In the past, both the child and the parents could use the child's exemption.

There were other significant changes which affected colleges and college-bound students: students are now faced with additional taxable income if they are recipients of fellowships, scholarships, and certain awards. Whatever amount of the scholarship or grant that is *not* spent on tuition and course-required equipment is now considered taxable income. In other words, any scholarship or grant funds spent on room, board, or incidental expenses are no longer excludable from income.

Parents were especially targeted for "reform." Heretofore income shifting was both legal and respectable to lower tax bills and save for college. The one vehicle that was routinely used to shift income was the Clifford trust, a short-term reversionary trust. The principal or assets in the trust reverted to the original grantor or donor after 10 years and 1 day.

Parents and grandparents, or anyone else who chose to, could fund the trust with cash, certificates of deposit, stocks, bonds, or other assets that produced income. The trust would then pay out the income to the beneficiaries of the trust, presumably the junior members of the family (although such a trust could be used for aged parents as well), who were obliged to pay income taxes on their benefits. If those assets had remained in the possession of the grantors, it was likely that the income would have been taxed at higher levels. The Clifford trust allowed for shifting of that income to the lowest tax rates.

The Clifford trust and other such arrangements were sharply curtailed by the introduction of the new "kiddie tax." This provision essentially taxes children's unearned income (interest from securities, savings, etc.) at their parents' rates until they are 14 years of age.

The law allows the first $1,200 of unearned income by a child under 14 years of age to be taxed at his or her rate. Any unearned income in excess of $1,200 will then be taxed at the parents' marginal rate. Any earned income in excess of the child's standard deduction would be taxed at his or her rate.

This effectively changed the savings patterns of parents of college-bound students. Some income-producing assets might be switched to a child since the first $600 escapes taxation completely, and the next $600 will be taxed at only 15 percent. But after that threshold, the parental rate governs for children's unearned income.

Parents have a choice as to whether to include the unearned income of their children on their own return, instead of filing separate returns for each child. But this election can be made only if your child's gross income consists solely of interest and dividends totaling no more than $5,000 and your child pays no estimated tax and is not subject to withholding.

This did not end income shifting, but it curtailed it dramatically, and made it more important than ever to plan just how to accumulate resources in the most efficient and cost-effective fashion, while avoiding undue taxes. This is especially true with the passage of the Revenue Reconciliation Act of 1993, which increased rates of taxation, especially for upper-bracket taxpayers. (See Appendix A.)

Furthermore, treatment of capital gains is an important aspect of a college savings program. This is especially significant since the top rate for long-term capital gains (the profit from the sale of assets held for at least one year) is only 28 percent, rather than the 31, 36, or 39.6 percent rates. Therefore, real after-tax savings are to be had by holding for long-term treatment. Any funds that can be converted from regular income to capital gains stand to benefit accordingly.

There are other tax provisions in the 1993 act that bear on investment decisions, such as the limit on investment interest deduction and limitations on pension contributions. For families with limited earned income, the new law expanded the earned income tax credit, thus reducing the tax bill.

It pays to examine these provisions in detail, since though they may not bear directly on college savings, they do have collateral implications for anyone trying to amass savings.

CHILDREN UNDER 14

The kiddie tax has long-term implications for college savers. It alters the nature of income shifting, especially if college planning is started early. Remember, it is income that is taxed, not capital growth. Thus one should follow a strategy of pursuing either growth or tax-free income when the children are young, that is from birth through their thirteenth year.

Four kinds of savings and/or investment vehicles are still valid to build wealth by way of income shifting:

1. U.S. savings bonds, EE series, now pay a minimum of 4 percent. That figure has been ratcheted down twice in the last decade, from 7.5 and 6 percent. Nevertheless, it compares quite favorably to certificates of deposit and other comparable savings instruments. At that rate, money will double in 18 years—thus the perfect instrument for the birth of a child destined for college.

The interest is not paid out on EE series bonds but accumulates and is paid on maturity. The gain or appreciation is then taxed by the federal government as ordinary income, but is not taxed by state and local governments.

When the EE bonds mature they can be rolled over into series HH bonds without payment of taxes. HH bonds pay taxable interest (also now 4 percent) semi-annually, but the tax liability from EE bonds does not come due until the HH bonds are redeemed or mature.

There is an additional advantage to U.S. savings bonds that is not available with other savings. They can now be used to pay college tuition, thus legally avoiding federal taxes on their appreciation. Bonds purchased beginning January 1, 1990, may be exempt on the interest income if their redemption proceeds are used for certain educational purposes.

Naturally, there are some limitations. The purchaser of the

bonds has to be at least 24 years of age. The proceeds from the sale of the bonds have to be used to pay for the qualified higher educational expenses of the purchaser, his or her spouse, or dependents.

This tax break phases out for married taxpayers filing jointly who have adjusted gross income of between $66,200 and $96,200. For single taxpayers and head of household filers, the range is $44,150 to $59,150. This tax break is not available if you are married filing separately.

2. Insurance policies, such as variable life and single premium life insurance, provide for tax-deferred growth. The so-called inside buildup of cash value is not taxed on a current basis. Therefore, income is earned on the original payment, on the earned accumulation, and on the portion that would have been paid in taxes.

3. Tax-exempt municipal bonds in a child's name will provide tax-free income, usually paid twice a year. The bonds can be bought with maturity dates that match college tuition payments. One problem with municipal bonds, other than the fact that they are difficult to buy singly or in odd lots, is that the twice-yearly payments of interest must be reinvested in other tax-free investments in order to avoid possible taxation. Parents should consider tax-free municipal bond funds. The yields are lower than other investments, but it is easier to buy shares in a bond fund than the bonds themselves if you are investing relatively small sums. Such tax-free funds also solve the problem of reinvestment of interest. Another development, motivated by the 1986 tax code, is the introduction of zero-coupon municipal bonds. These deep discounted bonds pay no semi-annual interest; the interest or yield accumulates at a given annual rate and the bonds are redeemed at par or face value in the year that they mature.

4. Growth stocks or a growth stock mutual fund should be part of a child's college tuition account. Traditionally, growth stocks pay little or no dividend income because these types of companies are using all their earnings to maximize their niche in the marketplace. What one loses in dividend income one hopes to gain in capital appreciation of the common stock's value. Such companies must be chosen with care since they may be more volatile than seasoned companies. A growth fund might be an alternative to individual selection. In either case, the tax conse-

quences are realized only after the shares are sold. If they are sold after the child reaches 14, then the child's lower tax rate will prevail rather than that of the parents.

CHILDREN OVER 14

When a child reaches age 14, interest, dividends, and capital gains will all be taxed as his or her earnings. They no longer will be taxed at the parent's rate, but at the child's independent rate. Thus anyone saving for college has from three or four years to seven or eight years (through the college years) to accumulate savings at relatively low rates.

At that point savers should shift their strategy from growth to income. Perhaps half of their savings pool should be targeted for high-interest income and half for capital growth. Though taxable income falls into one of three brackets for most taxpayers, no difference will exist in the source of earnings, be it income, interest, or short-term capital gains.

Remember that funds in a child's name will be weighed more heavily than funds in a parent's name in calculating financial aid needs. How then does one know whether to save in the name of a child or in the parent's name, before or after age 14, if the family is expecting some financial aid from the college? The worksheets and tables in Appendix E can help you estimate financial need as well as expected family contribution toward college costs.

If the likelihood of financial aid is remote, then it may be advantageous to keep most funds in the parent's name. Parents whose children may not get or even need financial aid may well need loans to complete a child's higher education and possible postgraduate work in order not to deplete their own savings. Therefore, the stronger the balance sheet parents can show, the more creditworthy they are considered by lenders. If one's assets are in other people's names—children, parents, joint or co-ownership with (nonfamily) others—creditors will be reluctant to provide loans.

6

TRUSTS AND LOANS

Learn to give
Money to colleges while you live.
Don't be silly and think you'll try
To bother the colleges, when you die
With codicil this, and codicil that,
That Knowledge may starve
** while Law grows fat.**
Oliver Wendell Holmes
The Autocrat of the Breakfast Table

Increasingly, a number of parents have turned to the use of trust instruments to overcome the problem of retaining control of the funds after the minority (usually 18 years of age) of the child has ended and to assure that the funds will be used for educational purposes. The other problem with gifts and loans is that they may not be used for certain complex financial investments. While trusts are more complicated and more costly to establish, they can provide greater security and flexibility in the long run.

The 1986 Tax Reform Act did reduce the tax benefits of trust instruments. They are no longer quite the tax shelters they were under the old code. However, they may still have a place in some strategies for conserving money for college, and for the years after the children finish college.

Before exploring the various types of trusts that may be used for saving money and preparing for college costs, it would be helpful to understand the basic nature of trust investments. Most people think of trusts as testamentary instruments, legal documents obligating an executor to parcel out the deceased's property. There are, however, a variety of living trusts, *inter vivos* trusts, which need not be posthumously operative—you don't have to die in order to use a trust instrument. Trusts can be as different and as varied as the creators would like to make them, though they generally fall into three categories: the testamentary trust; the irrevocable living trust; and the revocable living trust. Regardless of their purposes, the mechanics of all trusts are relatively similar.

Every trust must have four principals, though these may not necessarily be separate individuals. The individual who establishes the trust is known as the grantor or settlor, although the terms donor or maker are also used. The grantor may also be called the testator if the trust is established by his or her will. Naturally, a trust is made for someone's (or something's) benefit, who is formally known as the beneficiary—this is what a trust is all about. If there is no beneficiary, there is no trust. The third necessary office in any given trust arrangement is the trustee. A trustee can be an individual or an incorporated body such as a bank or professional organization. The trustee takes legal title to the property and henceforth is responsible for its productive investment for the sake of the beneficiary.

Finally, no trust is complete until a remainderman is chosen. Upon the termination of the trust (and all personal trusts must end), the property must be disposed of. It may or may not go to the beneficiary, depending on the terms of the trust. Whoever it is, the final inheritor of the trust property is known as the remainderman/woman. It is possible for the original grantor to appoint himself as the remainderman, but that of course would not be a testamentary trust. As noted, these four positions can be mixed and matched: The beneficiary can be the remainderman; the beneficiary can sometimes be the trustee; the grantor can be the beneficiary or the remainderman; and so on. While there is no simple definition of all trusts, a trust can be described generally as a fiduciary relationship between the parties—property is held by someone for the benefit and use of another. To make the trust a valuable instrument is the responsibility of the trustee, who must manage the property productively for the benefit of the trust and the beneficiary. The trustee keeps control of the assets, preserves the property, enforces claims that may constitute part of the trust, defends it from attack, and finally is responsible and accountable for what he or she does. The trustee, whether an individual or an organization, cannot delegate these powers, but is responsible for performing them. It goes without saying that a trustee should not use the position for personal enrichment and should avoid any position of conflict.

All of the living trusts that shall be discussed—Minors trust for children [under the IRS code termed a 2503 (c) trust], the Clifford trust, the Crummey trust, and the charitable-remainder trust—are based on the ability to shift income legally and properly. In order to facilitate that, the trust instruments require the grantor or donor to give up the right to control the principal and income of the trust, or the right to receive any benefit from the trust for the period of its duration. Consequently, it is of the utmost importance to appoint a trustee who is sympathetic with the donor's or grantor's wishes. The main purpose of all these trusts is to generate income in a lower tax bracket than that of the donors and pay out to the beneficiary to assist in tuition payments. However, if the corpus or principal of the trust is poorly managed, that action can be devastating and undermine the purpose of the trust, even if the trust complies with all the legal rules and obstacles. With the 1986 change in the tax code, shrewd management of funds is perhaps more important than the type of tax format or trust vehicle.

MINORS TRUST [2503 (C) TRUST]

One of the most common trusts to establish is the Minors trust, so named after the appropriate section of the Internal Revenue Code that describes it. The trust rules must be spelled out in a legal document; therefore, an attorney must be used in its creation. The parent or grantor establishes the trust by naming a child (or children) as beneficiary and providing the trustee with a gift of funds. Additional funds can be added as time goes by and in subsequent years. The trustee is charged with all the investment decisions, fulfilling the terms of the trust, and distributing income from the trust to the child. As a rule, the parent should not be the trustee, and the trust instrument should specifically state that the parent may not benefit from the funds in any way, nor use them to satisfy any parental obligations of support. Should the donor exercise any control of the trust property, income from the assets will be taxed to the donor.

The purpose of this Minors trust, as with most trusts, is to shift income from a high tax bracket to a low one and to extend control over the money beyond the age of 18, which is the usual age of majority under the Uniform Gifts to Minors Act.

Under the 2503 (c) trust, income from the trust property can accumulate in the trust and is taxed at the parent's tax rate until the child reaches the age of 14 (see Appendix C). The trust is not taxed on the income that it disburses during the course of the year. After the child reaches age 14, the income is taxed at the child's rate.

This type of trust can distribute *only* interest income during the years preceding age 21—in other words, during the usual college years the recipient would receive only interest income from the trust. When the beneficiary reaches 21 years of age, there are one of three possibilities:

- The trust is terminated and the child receives all the re-maining assets.

- The trust is terminated and the principal is returned to the parents or grantors.

- The principal may remain in trust for the child after 21 if he or she chooses to leave the trust intact.

In the latter option, the beneficiary has 60 days to withdraw the funds; otherwise the funds will be kept in trust, thus giving the trustee control of the funds beyond age 21.

The reason for the trust is primarily to maintain control of the funds beyond the time the beneficiary reaches age 18. Under the Uniform Gifts to Minors Act account, the custodian is required to terminate the account upon the child's majority and turn over the funds to him or her. Also, under a UGMA account, only certain types of property can be administered. In a trust, virtually any kind of property may be administered.

THE CLIFFORD TRUST

The Clifford trust allowed the grantors or parents to have their cake and eat it too under the old revenue act. A short-term irrevocable trust, it was set up to have the contributed assets taxed at a lower rate—either at that of the beneficiary or the trust. Shifting income in this way clearly saved tax money. It also guaranteed the grantor's control of the assets; since the Clifford trust is a reversionary trust, all property reverts to the grantor's ownership 10 years and 1 day after being deposited in the trust.

As previously noted, the 1986 tax code eliminated tax saving through asset shifting because all unearned or investment income in excess of $1,000 for children under age 14 is taxed at their parents' rate, regardless of source. Clifford trusts established before March 1, 1986, will be taxed at the parent's tax rate regardless of when they were established. Any property transferred to any Clifford trust (and the income therefrom), whether established before or after March 1, 1986, will be taxed to the grantor.

Though the Clifford trust has lost much of its appeal, it may still have some use. If established and funded for the benefit of a child after his or her fourteenth birthday, the trust can generate income at the child's tax rate if the trust's income is distributed to the child, and a child's unearned income is likely to be in a lower bracket than the income of the parent. On the other hand, the income should be distributed rather than retained in the trust since the applicable rate for trusts is 28 percent for income over $5,000. Too much property in a Clifford trust would be counterproductive.

Perhaps the major concern for parents considering the Clifford trust is not income shifting, but control. It does provide a means for setting up a custodial college fund without turning those assets over to the child. If the assets are given outright, without benefit of the trust, the tax savings will be similar, but the parents lose control of the funds upon the child's majority.

There is a tendency to use friendly trustees in Clifford trusts.

This can be a dangerous step; it is best if the trustee is independent and a professional asset manager. If a family member is used as trustee, then the trust instrument should be specific as to beneficiary, income distribution, and accumulation by the trust. If the trustee is independent (that is, in no position subservient to the donor), then it is beneficial to give him or her as much leeway as possible in administering the trust. Since the trust is to run for at least 10 years, it is wise to have a provision to provide for the change of trustees if the trustee is performing poorly.

The basic use of Clifford trusts is for educational purposes, though they may be used in other circumstances as well. Presuming that the child's college expenses will be relatively equal each year, the trust will pay out of its income the interest that accumulates from its assets. The trust assets can be varied: interest-bearing bonds, savings accounts, mutual funds, and money-market accounts. It is also possible to give equities, property, real estate interests, and interests in businesses. Presumably the income thrown off by these assets will cover a significant portion of college expenses. A trustee, depending on the rules of the trust, may pass all of that income to the student or invest the proceeds to earn more income. The income passed to the student will be taxed at the student's tax rate, while the income accumulated to the trust will be taxed at its slightly higher trust rate. If the accumulated income of the trust is not distributed to the beneficiaries in one year or in subsequent years, it must be paid over to them when the trust terminates.

Whatever property is transferred to the trust, it is the job of the trustee to administer the property productively. If securities or an interest in a business is given as part of the trust assets, there may be a time during the life of the trust when those assets should be sold or a business terminated. If so, the capital gains or losses in the trust could be offset by gains or losses outside the trust. Since the grantor has a reversionary interest in the property, any capital gains or losses are not taxed to the trust but to the grantor. Consequently, a capital gains within the trust would produce a tax consequence unless there was an offsetting capital loss inside or outside the trust. A trust that produces a capital gain without an offsetting loss will cause the grantor to be taxed on a gain he or she will not be able to receive until the trust is ended. While any property can be placed in a Clifford trust, it is probably best to include only assets that can be bought and sold without any significant tax consequence.

While the duration of the normal Clifford trust is 10 years and 1 day after the transmission of the property to the trust, there is a short-term Clifford trust that enables the trust to be terminated in a briefer period if the remainderman/woman is not the grantor. This is called the spousal remainder trust. All the other rules of the Clifford trust apply: The grantor's spouse can be designated to receive the property at the end of a five-year period. Nor will there be any adverse gift tax consequences since there is an unlimited marital deduction for gifts. But this short-term arrangement is based on the fact that the reversionary interest to the spouse (or someone else) is indeed a true gift—one without strings. Under the tax code, the spousal remainder trust is taxed in the same way as the Clifford trust.

THE CRUMMEY TRUST

Another irrevocable trust named for another tax case is the Crummey, or independent, trust. The major difference between it and the Minors trust is that it may last beyond the age of 21, extending as long as the beneficiary's lifetime. The trustee is given discretion to pay out income or accumulate funds in line with the beneficiary's needs. This trust is subject to the same general constraints as noted above for other trusts: The annual gift made by the donor can be up to $10,000 for gift tax exclusion; the income to the trust is taxed to the beneficiary (when he or she is over age 14) when it is paid out or taxed to the trust if it is not distributed; the trustee can be anyone, although it is preferable that he or she be independent; there are no restraints on the kind of property given to the trust. Beneficiaries of trusts are taxed on their share of trust income, whether paid out or not. There is never a double tax. Finally, remember that each item of trust income is treated the same for the beneficiary as it is for the trust.

There are some differences, however: This independent trust has no required termination date, only one assigned by the grantor of the trust; unlike other trusts, the beneficiary must have the power to withdraw funds from the trust once a year for a limited period, but there is no requirement to do so. Therefore, the trust can accumulate income long after the beneficiary reaches his or her majority or the age of 21. Unlike the Clifford trust, when the Crummey trust terminates, the remaining principal is paid to the beneficiary rather than reverting to the donor or grantor. The Crummey trust is somewhat more flexible than other trusts, allowing for accumulation of funds if they are not withdrawn and then disbursed by the trustee at his or her discretion. Since educational needs often continue past the age of 21, especially if postgraduate work is envisioned, the Crummey trust will provide for individual needs of different beneficiaries.

There is one other interesting difference between the Crummey and the Clifford trusts in that with the Crummey trust, capital gains and losses are taxed to the trust or to the beneficiary, depending on whether they are accumulated or distributed, rather than to the grantor or parent. Sales of appreciated property may be beneficial in a Crummey trust since the capital-gains tax for the beneficiary or child is likely to be lower than for the grantor or parent. On the other hand, the beneficiary or child may not be able to use a capital loss as expeditiously as the donor or parent.

CHARITABLE-REMAINDER TRUST

Finally, there is a charitable-remainder trust: Gifts to the trust are a charitable deduction to those who itemize deductions, since the principal will be contributed to a charity when the trust ends. While the beneficiary or child is attending college, income from the trust will be applied to tuition expenses. Upon the establishment of the trust, the grantor or parent can designate either a fixed income from the trust to the beneficiary or a fixed percentage of the assets as they accumulate annually. Naturally, any income to the child is taxable to him or her after the age of 14. Contrary to other trusts, accumulated income is not taxed since the assets will eventually be contributed to charity, which is frequently the attended college or university.

7

BUSINESS AND COLLEGE COSTS

HIRE YOUR CHILD

There are over 14 million small businesses in the United States, most of them privately owned by families. Business entities are favorably treated under the tax code, and family businesses can participate in a number of benefits that will assist in meeting educational costs. There are some rulings and provisions in the tax code that give specific and targeted assistance to small-business owners to ease the educational costs of their children. In addition, by using some of the general and routine deductions and expenses derived from standard accounting practices, it is possible to obtain substantial educational savings.

Some of the following techniques may help in lowering taxable income while at the same time providing income to children to assist in paying college costs. These techniques are not ploys to coax more financial assistance from the colleges. Nor are they meant to deceive financial aid officers as to the true value of a family business in appraising financial need. Indeed, most colleges will require an additional Financial Aid Form, or a Business/Farm Supplement in order to determine a fair net worth for a wholly-owned family business or farm or for a partially owned one. Therefore, the following information should be understood in that context.

Perhaps first and foremost is the simple step of employing your child in some work capacity. The law, of course, neither encourages nor discourages parents from hiring their children. Children can be hired on a full-time or part-time basis. The practice is clearly self-serving, but perfectly legal. Their pay or salary then becomes an ordinary and necessary business expense—one fully deductible from the expense side of the ledger. The business has accomplished presumably what it would have had to do in any circumstance, and paid someone to do it. Instead of money leaving the family, it remains within the family circle. The child is then able to bank his or her salary, using the earned money for college costs.

For example, a father who owns a lumberyard hires his teenage son as a laborer to load and unload inventory. He pays his son a laborer's wage, $5 per hour, for 600 hours of work—a total of $3,000. The business has incurred a cost of $3,000, thus simultaneously lowering its taxable income. If the parent, as sole proprietor, is in the 28 percent tax bracket, he has saved $840 he otherwise would have had to pay in personal income tax.

The son, besides exercising his muscles and using his time, has gained $3,000 of income that is virtually tax free since it falls within his standard deduction. The father has saved either paying an outsider or exerting himself, while the son is able to save his total pay. If the business is incorporated, then the father would be obliged to pay social security tax on his son's labor, as he would with any other employee. But even that can be waived if the son has no intention of earning enough money to be obliged to pay taxes.

There are a couple of warnings about family hiring. If the expenses for the business are *not* ordinary and necessary, they will not be deductible. It strains the imagination for a lumberyard to hire a photographer, short-order cook, or lifeguard, but it is perfectly reasonable for it to hire a carpenter, laborer, or truck driver. Any expense that is clearly irrelevant will be struck down by the IRS.

Furthermore, while a management consultant or a psychoanalyst might command $100 per hour, a day laborer does not. Pay or salary must be commensurate with the activity. If children are being hired to sweep the yard, do the laundry, and shop for groceries, the minimum wage is probably appropriate.

Besides appropriate pay and job (don't send a boy to do a man's work, in the words of the old saw), parental hiring should be formalized with a written record of employment, and payment should be made by way of a check. It makes no difference if the business is a sole proprietorship, partnership, S corporation, or ordinary corporation. Moreover, the same rules are applicable to professions as well: Doctors, lawyers, dentists, and engineers can just as easily hire their children in some appropriate capacity.

EDUCATIONAL FRINGE BENEFITS

Some businesses have set up elaborate fringe benefits to help with the educational costs of their owners' children. This is a complicated procedure and such benefits have to go to all employees. It may well be more expensive than originally anticipated. Furthermore, the IRS monitors such benefits to see that they are not on the face of it discriminatory, favoring owners or senior management. Nevertheless, it is perfectly legitimate for businesses to establish an educational-assistance program. Under such a program, the business may pay for tuition, fees, books, course supplies, and similar items. Payments have been deductible as business expenses but not includable in the gross income of the employees. Nor have these payments been subject to FICA (Federal Insurance Contributions Act, which withholds for social security) or FUTA (Federal Unemployment Tax Act) deductions.

If the firm does have an educational-assistance plan that meets the qualifying requirements (as noted below), up to $5,250 of assistance to each employee yearly can be excluded from reportable income. Any amount in excess of $5,250 must be included as wages in the employee's income as reported to the government on W-2 forms. This excess is subject to income tax withholding, FICA and FUTA.

A qualified educational-assistance program must fulfill the following requirements:

- It must have a separate written plan from an employer for the exclusive benefit of the employees to give them educational assistance.

- It cannot have eligibility requirements that discriminate in favor of officers, owners, or highly compensated employees or their dependents.

- It may not expend more than 5 percent of the amounts paid or incurred for educational assistance on a shareholder or owner (or his or her spouse or dependents) who (on any day of the year) owns more than 5 percent of the stock or of the capital or profits interest in the employing company.

- It must not provide eligible employees with a choice between educational assistance and other remuneration includable in gross income.

- It need not be funded.

- It must provide for reasonable notification of the availability and the terms of the program to eligible employees.

If there is no formal program and the business pays for tuition expenses of employees who are enrolled in courses that are not required for their jobs or are not otherwise related, then the IRS expects these payments to be treated as wages. In short, they are includable in income and are subject to FICA and FUTA payments.

Some corporations, especially professional corporations, have formally established educational-benefit trusts (EBTs). The corporation sets aside funds for the EBT, which annually accumulates additional funds on a tax-free basis from investments. When the qualifying children of employees reach the required age, funds are then paid out for their educational expenses. The employees are, of course, the nominal owners of the corporation as well.

To be eligible as an EBT, the plan must:

- Cover all employees, not just a few

- Be a fringe benefit, not a substitute for true compensation

- Involve a trust administered or managed by an independent trustee

- Be set up so that the business does not stand to gain from reversion of the funds or control of them

CHILDREN AS PARTNERS

Educational fringe benefits were an excellent way for a business to pay for tuition costs. However, if there were additional employees other than the immediate family, it turned out to be rather expensive extending those benefits to all employees. The 1986 tax code limited those educational benefits. Consequently, many small family businesses have turned to another way to finesse educational costs—by making the children partners. They are then legitimately entitled to their share of the profits—or even losses.

There is one special caveat that bears repeating: Disclosure of ownership of assets, in its broadest sense, is required in application for financial aid (for example, in the Financial Aid Form of the College Scholarship Service of the College Board, the Application for Federal Student Aid of the Department of Education, the Family Financial Statement of the American College Testing Program). The more assets in a youngster's name, the greater the assessment when a dependent student files for aid. A dependent student will have approximately 35 percent of his or her assets assessed for tuition costs while the parents are assessed between 5 and 12 percent of their assets. If financial aid is going to be applied for, it is probably wise to have assets in the parents' rather than the child's name. But if the family is relatively well off, rich in assets, and with an income of over $50,000, the chances for substantial assistance are not good. The family will have to balance the after-tax savings of gifts and business interests against educational assistance. For an upper-middle-income family, one with its own business, the tax advantages are likely to be greater than the financial assistance they would receive.

Transferring a business interest is a perfectly legal device to both reduce taxes and increase college funding. There are, however, a number of reservations and conditions that must be strictly observed. Clearly, a consultation with a lawyer, accountant, and/or financial adviser is a necessity in order to avoid traps and mistakes.

There are four types of business organizations: sole proprietorship, partnership, S corporation, and ordinary corporation. For the purposes of taxation, the first three are all taxed in the same way. In general, whatever income is left after all expenses are paid is considered profit. All the profits, and the losses, flow through to the owner, or partners, or shareholders in an S corporation (so named after a section in the revenue code), so that they are taxed as individual, personal income. This arrangement allows for some flexibility in using a business's income as educational funds. Incorporated businesses, as we shall see, have less leeway in splitting profits.

A family business that is a sole proprietorship can easily be made into a partnership, or an existing partnership can increase the number of partners to accommodate one or more children. The children, even if they are still minors, can thereby share in the profits. They are then, naturally, liable for taxes on their profits and will be obliged to file an income tax return and an information return from the partnership, even though the partnership itself pays no taxes.

Partners may or may not be of equal standing: Two partners may have a fifty–fifty share of the business or a ninety–ten arrangement. Their profits will be split accordingly. This will hold true for most commonplace businesses, from service stations to newsstands, from shoe stores to printing shops. It will *not* hold true for professional service organizations, even if the new partner has made a cash contribution to the business. Doctors and lawyers, for example, cannot assign their service income to others— they must pay taxes on such income personally.

Service fees and commissions do not necessarily prohibit a partner from receiving a distribution of the family business, but the income from services must be deducted before partnership distribution is made. Then the remaining profit can rightly be viewed as a return on capital, which is necessary for brick, mortar, and inventory. The IRS is concerned about two points:

- A family member's share should be determined after allowing for reasonable compensation for services rendered to the partnership by the donor.

- A share of the profit allocated to the family member donee must be proportional—it should not be greater than the share of the donor attributable to the donor's capital.

For the vast majority of small businesses, those that are either labor intensive or capital intensive and in which labor and capital are necessary for producing income, shifting income to partners is permissible. Indeed, it is mandatory to proportionately shift income to the new partner if the arrangement is not to be regarded as a sham. The child-partner may either purchase an interest in the business or be given it as a gift. Both are acceptable ways of creating a partner. As with all gifts, whether to the child or to his or her custodian or trustee, the gift must be complete and irrevocable.

This partnership arrangement must be formalized by assessing or evaluating the interest, drawing up a deed or title to the interest, creating partnership papers (or transferring a partnership interest if it is already an ongoing business), and registering them with local authorities. Records must be kept and tax forms filed. A true partnership interest also means that it can be sold by the child when he or she reaches maturity or through his or her guardian or trustee before that time. This may create a problem in a small family business, but it is perhaps more a problem in theory than in practice, since minority outside interests in a family business are likely to be few. A trustee should be independent, though friendly, since it enhances the independence of the arrangement. A Clifford trust would not be an acceptable partner since its reversionary nature (property in a Clifford trust reverts to the grantor 10 years and 1 day after it was contributed) defies the prime characteristics of a true gift.

S CORPORATIONS AND ORDINARY CORPORATIONS

The S corporation retains the major ingredient of a corporation in that it provides limited liability. However, if a corporation elects for S status, it will be able to pass on all profits and losses to the shareowners. Indeed, the income retains its original character—income, interest, or capital gains. In short, it is taxed as a partnership, not as a corporation. S corporations are difficult and complicated to establish and maintain, and are only good for active or operating corporations. If the corporation has passive income (rents, royalties, dividends, foreign income) totaling more than 25 percent, or more than 35 stockholders, or more than one class of shares, the corporation is ineligible to become an S corporation.

However, if a corporation elects to do so, it is possible to give (or sell) a stockholder's interest to a child. This interest may be held by a child over 18 years of age, by a minor through a custodian or guardian, or by a special trust called a qualified S trust. A portion of the profits of the corporation can be shifted, after allowing for all service salaries, and paid to the child, who in turn must pay income tax. The advantage, as noted in the previous section, is that the procedure shifts income from the high-bracket parent, who owned 100 percent of the stock, to the low-bracket child (or trust), who now owns some fractional interest of the corporation. The monies can then be invested and accumulated while awaiting college. S corporations are complicated instruments and can be disallowed by the IRS for a variety of reasons. Professional advice should be sought in order to avoid the mine fields.

It is no less complicated with closely held corporations. Take the case of parents who jointly own a corporation of the ordinary kind. One of the great benefits of being incorporated, besides limited liability, is the ability to pay out or not pay out profits, within limitations. A corporation may accumulate $150,000 if it provides services; it may accumulate $250,000 if it produces goods. Sums accumulated beyond that limit will be taxed unless they are assigned for specific purposes. The parents can play out a couple of scenarios.

First of all, they can give their child a minor interest in the company—say 10 percent of the stock, or 10 shares. He or she would then receive a proportionate amount of dividends distributed by the corporation. If the parents declared a dividend of $500 per share, the child would receive $5,000. This sum would be taxed as regular income. But this might present a problem for the parents, since they might not wish to be taxed personally on the other 90 percent ($45,000) worth of dividends at that time.

The second possibility allows for a distribution of dividends to the child without the parents necessarily paying themselves. This can be done by recapitalizing the corporation—issuing another class of common or preferred shares. The parents can declare as little dividend income as they wish on the founders' shares, but a different rate of payout on Class B or preferred shares. While there are some tax considerations, this technique does allow for a payout to a child or trust. Recapitalizing or distributing assets, whether for cash or as a gift of a closely held corporation, raises the question of valuation and control: How much are the shares worth? This in turn leads to the next question: Are they subject to a gift tax? Tax, estate, and gift considerations are all part of splitting business income. As far as control is concerned, issuing a nonvoting class of stock ensures that the parents retain ownership of the corporation no matter how many children are given nonvoting shares.

If carefully pursued, businesses can provide educational funds to children from a relatively low tax base. The cost does not reduce the corporate tax since dividends are paid with after-tax monies, but it does allow income to accumulate in a custodian or trust account.

The tax laws, as noted on several other occasions, restrict the parents' ability to lower the effective tax rate on investment income by transferring assets to a child. It is the net unearned income (over $1,000) of a child under age 14 that is taxed as if it were a parent's income. A child's earned income, however, is taxed at a child's rate. The 1986 tax law changes were clearly intended to tax interest and investment income that parents had transferred to their children. However, property given to a child, such as a share in a business, is a true gift for federal tax purposes. Therefore, any income generated from property transferred under these procedures is taxable to the child, unless it is used in any way to satisfy a legal obligation of support of that child.

BUSINESS GIFTS AND LEASEBACKS

Businesses and professions require any number of items to be productive, from cars to computers, from office space to silo space. As long as there is a legitimate business or investment need, there is a legitimate way of transferring that equipment or item to a child's trust and leasing it from the trust for business use. This leaseback arrangement can provide substantial tax reductions while furnishing educational funds or income to one's children.

The IRS, to be sure, will look critically at an intra-family arrangement, as they do with family trusts generally. However, if properly constructed and for a real business purpose, it should pass muster. Giving and leasing back mom's microwave oven is *not* a real transaction, but one involving a ceramic kiln for a potter would certainly be appropriate.

As with the transfer of a partnership business interest or shares of a closely held family corporation, the simplest way is to give to a child's trust the business or professional property that is required in one's trade. Through a formal written agreement, the trust then turns around and leases the property back to the businessperson or professional for a reasonable market rent. While the trustee should be friendly, he or she should not be subservient in any way. In brief, the trustee should be independent and the trust an irrevocable one. Since the gift is a substantial one, it must be fairly evaluated. Perhaps a gift tax will have to be paid if it exceeds in value the unified credit.

While the leaseback arrangement can be used with new equipment, it is probably a better deal with used and/or fully depreciated capital equipment. For example, a professional writer purchased a word processor five years ago for $15,000. It has been fully depreciated to the point where its depreciation basis is $3,000. In the open market, the machine is worth $5,000. The writer donates the equipment, fairly evaluated at $5,000, to his teenager's trust. No gift tax applies since it is below the annual $10,000 limitation. For the trust, the basis price is the depreciated value of $3,000, a figure that must be used in the trust's tax calculations. The trust then leases the word processor back to the writer for a rent of $300 monthly, or $3,600 for the year. The $3,600 is income to the child's trust; the nominal tax at the 15 percent rate will be $540. For the parent in the 28 percent tax bracket, the tax saving on the $3,600 is $1,008, and the total tax saving is almost $470 per year. The trust has a steady source of income and the parent, a substantial tax saving. After a number of years, the trust will be able to make a notable contribution to the child's college costs.

Borrowing from Your Retirement Plan

Not all parents are professionals, self-employed, or owners of a family corporation from which they may take advantage of the various tax benefits and advantages given to small businesses. However, almost everyone has some sort of retirement or pension savings program, whether they are self-employed or employed by a corporation. Since the Employee Retirement Act of 1974, which protected the interest of workers, there has been a growing movement to establish, regulate, and guarantee pension funds. These funds are now enormous pools of money that are invested for the benefit of employees as they retire. Under some special circumstances, these funds are available to employees during their working careers: Employees can in essence borrow their own money.

All retirement plans, in order to receive the tax benefits accorded to them, must be either with the employing company or with an authorized custodian such as a bank, trust company, brokerage house, mutual fund, or insurance company. Three kinds of retirement plans are generally available: the Individual Retirement Account (IRA), Keogh plans, and 401 (k) or salary-reduction plans. They can overlap, and some individuals are eligible for all three.

Individual Retirement Account

Originally, an individual retirement account could be opened and maintained by anyone. Today the IRA is limited in its benefits. It still allows for an annual maximum deposit of $2,000 ($2,250 for joint-filing spouses where only one works), but this sum is deductible from taxable income only if one is not covered by a qualified company pension plan or profit-sharing plan, or if one has an adjusted gross income of $25,000 or less ($40,000 for joint filers). Furthermore, if one has an adjusted gross income of between $25,000 and $35,000 ($40,000 and $50,000 for joint filers), a portion of the contribution may be deductible. Those individuals who had established IRAs under the old code but are no longer eligible for tax deductions of their contributions may still continue contributing. While the contribution is not tax deductible, it may still earn interest in an IRA account on a tax-deferred basis until withdrawn.

Provided that the account is with an authorized custodian, a wide variety of investment options are available. Funds in an IRA compound without facing any taxation until they are withdrawn.

The funds are available after 59.5 years of age, but must be withdrawn before 70.5 years of age. They will then be taxed as ordinary income.

It is not impossible to tap one's IRA for college funds. However, only two considerations have been established by the government to allow for withdrawal of monies without penalty before age 59.5: (1) If you become physically or mentally incapacitated, or (2) if you die, the funds can be withdrawn by your beneficiaries. If you wish to invade the IRA before age 59.5 for any other reason, the government will tax the withdrawal and penalize you 10 percent. While many advisers recommend that you avoid tapping the IRA, it may well be worthwhile if funds have been accumulating rapidly due to aggressive investment policies. Knowledgeable or well-advised individuals can have self-directed IRA accounts. They need not settle for money-market or certificate-of-deposit rates but may, instead, take any portion of their funds for equity investments. Thus, if the IRA has grown prodigiously, that growth will more than likely offset the penalty. While this may be somewhat unconventional, it is assuredly a source of college monies. With a maximum IRA contribution of $2,000 per year, the monies compounded daily at 8 percent will result in the following sums:

Annual contribution	In 5 years	In 10 years	In 20 years
$2,000	$13,000	$32,000	$103,000

Keogh Plans

Keogh plans are similar to IRAs. Anyone, whether employed or self-employed, may start an IRA, even if he or she has a company pension account as well. Originally, Keoghs were only for the self-employed. Starting in 1985, Keoghs were broadened to include small and professional corporations. A self-employed person, a professional corporation, or a small business may contribute to a Keogh account. The actual contribution can be made only after deducting that contribution from net earnings, so the result is somewhat lower than it would first appear. The contribution, however, is deductible against personal income. (It is also possible to make an extra voluntary contribution of up to 10 percent of self-employed income, but that portion is *not* deductible.)

The funds compound on a tax-free basis. Taxes are paid only upon commencement of withdrawal at age 59.5 or later, depending on whether you have a profit-sharing plan or a money-purchase plan. Should you decide to withdraw your funds in a lump sum, you may take advantage of a five-year averaging formula that spreads the tax liability over five years. As with IRAs, funds may not be withdrawn without penalty unless disability or death occurs. However, it is possible to have a self-directed Keogh as long as it is with an authorized custodian. You may then invade the plan for college expenses, but you will be penalized by incurring taxable income and a 10 percent penalty tax. Still, if the plan has been operating successfully for a substantial period of time, the penalty need not be too onerous.

401 (k) or Salary-Reduction Plans

Finally, an employer pension set up under section 401 (k) of the IRS code provides for a generous salary-reduction plan. These pension plans are also known as deferred-payment plans or income-savings plans, since whatever the employees contribute reduces taxable income by that amount before social security taxes. In addition, the employer frequently adds a significant contribution that is credited to the employee's account and becomes part of that account when the employee becomes fully vested. Again, as with IRAs and Keoghs, the contributions compound tax free until retirement or until withdrawn. Employees now may put only up to $8,475 of their salary into a salary-reduction plan.

Salary-reduction plans are particularly appealing for parents in search of college funds. Under most plans—regardless of how they are invested, be it company stock, mutual funds, or money-market accounts—it is possible to borrow from one's own contributions, but not without penalty. The regulations will of course differ from company to company, but in general you may withdraw your funds (pleading hardship, which usually includes college tuition) before retiring. Under the tax code, however, such withdrawals are penalized 10 percent, and income tax must be paid if the original contribution was tax-deferred income.

The withdrawal can be structured as a loan. It is possible to

borrow at a low rate of interest, and *no* penalty tax is levied. The
interest payments are not tax deductible, but they are credited to
your own account as you pay back the loan. One drawback with
401 (k) plans is that the participant has little to say in how his or
her funds are to be invested, other than designating general categories such as stocks, fixed income, or mutual funds. Nevertheless, salary-reduction plans are certainly worthwhile for tax de-
ferral and certainly add to parental borrowing power if there is a
temporary shortage of funds.

8

BORROWING

PAY-AS-YOU-GO

Shakespeare's Polonius advised his son Laertes to be neither a borrower nor a lender. Reasonable advice, even though creditors today no longer demand a pound of flesh from overdue borrowers. Usury is also against the law, but high interest rates can certainly be painful. Therefore, it is important to weigh carefully borrowing options. For assuredly, most college students and parents of college students will avail themselves of some loan facility before college graduation. Today the average college student after four years of schooling is in debt to the tune of $10,000.

While that sounds like an onerous burden for someone just entering the job market, most lenders will structure a payback schedule over many years to ease the pain. But it is equally important to look at the other side of the balance sheet, at what you get for the cost of a college degree.

Two facts should be borne in mind:

1. The trend of wages and salaries in the 1980s and early 1990s is against high school (only) graduates. They not only make less money than college graduates, but relatively they are falling further and further behind as low-skilled jobs pay increasingly less money. And the corollary is that the likelihood of unemployment grows greater. College graduates now earn 57 percent more than those without degrees.

2. College may be expensive, but a glance at U.S. Census figures indicates that the career difference between high school and college graduates is dramatic. The average net worth of a household headed by someone with a high school diploma is $109,000, while the average net worth of a household headed by someone with a college degree is $364,600.

Borrowing funds is very much part of the modern capitalist economy—money is what makes the mare go. While the cost of credit is still a legitimate business expense, revisions of the tax code have now ruled out tax deductibility for consumer expenses. Just another reason for shopping for credit since you can no longer have the federal government share the expense of a loan by writing it off.

There are many different ways to borrow and a number of loan programs that parents and children-students may use to further their educational ends. When borrowing keep in mind:

- Interest rates are now at cyclical lows. Consequently there is a lot of competition among lenders. Shop around for the best terms.

- Consider adjustable-rate loans if they are offered instead of fixed-rate loans. In an environment of low inflation adjustable rates may save you money.

- Pay the loan(s) back in accordance with your own timetable, quickly if you have the funds or slowly if you do not.

- Most student loans do *not* give the borrower the option of refinancing them should interest rates drop precipitously. Therefore look for ones that do offer this choice, such as the Parent Loans to Undergraduate Students (PLUS).

- While it is premature to worry about repayment, bear in mind that there are steps that can be taken to defer, postpone, alter repayment schedules, and consolidate student loans—all legitimate ways for a graduate to deal with the burden of paying for college.

Parents generally fall into two categories: those who have prepared to pay college bills from the day their children were born, and the rest of us. Most of us save money, haphazardly or not, with the vague idea that some of those savings will be dedicated to our children's education. But the underlying idea is usually that we certainly will be more affluent and better paid when the kids are ready for school. Too often, college costs are put on a pay-as-you-go basis. College fees then have to be met along with all the other current expenses—food, mortgage, rent, or entertainment. This approach can be costly since it neglects some of the valuable money-saving ideas available to parents that are discussed elsewhere in this book. However, there are still a few steps that will save families some money even if college costs are paid out of current income.

LINES OF CREDIT

Everyone with a bank card such as Visa or MasterCard, among others, has an established line of credit—anywhere from $1,000 to $15,000. And some schools will accept payment through a bank card for tuition. However, this is a costly way to borrow money since, after the first billing cycle, the billing company will start charging interest. Interest rates frequently range from 8 to 18 percent. No one should finance college bills with a credit card, except for a short period of time or in dire emergencies.

Lines of credit are also implicit with most savings accounts. The most common is the passbook loan. By leaving your passbook account as collateral, banks and thrifts will, in essence, lend you back your own money. The bank will enjoy the advantage of the spread: It will pay you 3 percent on your passbook account while it lends you money at a much higher rate, say 8 percent.

Presumably you will not need the whole line of credit, which is the balance in the account, but will borrow only what is needed to bridge college costs. Repayment of the loan starts immediately, so that in three, five, or seven years the loan is totally repaid. Interest charges, before tax considerations, may well be a wash, that is, the interest earned on the greater amount of savings may match the interest costs of the loan. In essence, it is a free loan. Best of all, the passbook savings account or the principal remains intact when the loan is paid off. Your local bank can supply the details of a passbook or collateralized-loan line of credit. Under the tax code, earned interest is taxable, but interest charges are not deductible.

There are a number of commercial organizations and insurance companies, besides banks and thrifts, that provide lines of credit for college purposes. Essentially, they help parents budget their expenses: They prepay, either to the parents or to the college, the tuition fees and then bill the parents. Some claim that there are no interest costs, but remember that these are not eleemosynary institutions, and whatever the finance charges are called, they are indeed a form of interest. These organizations serve a purpose by providing lump-sum payments to the schools for parents who may be short of resources but have substantial incoming cash flows. They do charge a nominal participation fee for enrollment and often offer optional life insurance for parents. While the plans purportedly keep one out of debt—that is, from amassing a reportable liability—their assistance does not come cheaply. One popular tuition plan charges 17.5 percent as its annual percentage rate, which is roughly the same as a bank credit card. For example, under one plan for a one-year program*:

Amount financed	12 monthly payments	Total monthly payments
$5,000	$444.35	$5,332.20

* The interest rate is higher than it appears to be since you have had use of only half the principal for the whole year.

Some of the more popular educational loan programs are:

- The Tuition Plan, Donovan Street Extension, Concord, New Hampshire 03301; telephone 800-258-3640 or 603-228-1161

- Academic Management Services, 50 Vision Boulevard, East Providence, Rhode Island 02914; telephone 800-637-3060 or 401-431-1490

- University Support Services, 205 Van Buren Street, Herndon, Virginia 22070; telephone 800-767-5626

- The Education Resources Institute, 330 Stuart Street, Boston, Massachusetts 02116; telephone 800-255-8374

HOME EQUITY LOANS

The 1986 tax reform act left only one itemized deduction that home owners may use to help finance an education: the home equity loan. Besides primary mortgage interest, interest on second mortgages, or home equity loans, is still a deductible item against income. Renters of homes or apartments have no such deductions available to them and, of course, cannot apply for such loans.

Home equity loans may legitimately be used to pay costs such as home improvement and medical expenses. They also may be used to pay tuition by parents who either are forced, or prefer, to pay for college on a current basis. Under the tax code there are some limits to a home equity loan's interest deductibility: The total borrowed amount should not exceed the house's purchase price, plus the cost of improvements, regardless of the present appraised value. However, if one borrows more than the prescribed limit, but uses it only on educational costs (or medical costs), the deductibility is allowed.

Banks, of course, have their own limits. They often will establish a line of credit that equals somewhere between 50 and 75 percent of the current market value of the home or condominium. The home equity loan line of credit is calculated as follows when there is $50,000 outstanding on a first mortgage.

Present market value of home	$150,000
Maximum lending level	×75%
	112,500
Less mortgage balance	− 50,000
Maximum line of credit	$ 62,500

Another way of borrowing against your own money is to remortgage your home. Home equity loans have become exceedingly popular due to the rapid rise in real estate values in the seventies and early eighties. Many home owners longed to touch the equity that had built up over the years. The traditional way was (and is) to take out a second mortgage if the first was not completely paid for, but these were inflexible and expensive. Interest rates could range between 20 percent and 50 percent higher than the original mortgage.

In order to unleash all that paper wealth, financial institutions introduced a home equity loan—essentially a line of credit against one's residence. While such loans do not make sense for consumer items, since they are a form of consumption that will eventually eat up the equity, they can be used for college education. There are some considerable costs associated with opening this line of credit—an appraiser's fee, mortgage search, application processing—adding as much as 2 percent or more of the line of credit. In some instances, the fees are even higher.

Most important is the rate of interest for this type of loan. Since the early eighties, mortgage lenders have often insisted on adjustable- or variable-rate loans. Interest rates on the loans are tied to some general index such as Treasury bills, the prime rate, or the consumer price index. In brief, loans that are tied to such indices are subject to interest rate fluctuation, which may mean greater (or lesser) monthly charges. Should the economy go into a prolonged period of inflation, the increasing interest costs could be painful. As a rule, interest charges on variable-rate loans will be roughly in line with new mortgage rates, perhaps 1 or 2 percentage points lower.

Home equity loans are especially valuable for unlocking the incremental value of one's home. However, they can be a dangerous tool since the underlying collateral is the home. Should one fail to pay off the loan on time, for whatever reason, it could put the roof over your head in jeopardy. Finally, the loan becomes due immediately if the home is sold—again putting a strain on one's cash flow.

Economic conditions in the 1990s have altered the context for home equity loans. With the 1990–92 recession came a substantial drop in real estate prices—many homes bought in the second half of the 1980s now have a market value less than the purchase price. For such owners, the home equity loan may not be an option, especially if the size of the prime mortgage exceeds the market price of the home.

Nevertheless, owners of both older homes as well as those recently acquired can take a significant step in reducing their mortgage costs. Since interest rates are generally lower in the

1990s than they were in the previous decade, refinancing a high-interest mortgage may save several hundred dollars per month—dollars that could go toward tuition payments. This is a step not to be taken lightly since it entails going through the same steps as acquiring a mortgage in the first instance. However, a refinanced $100,000 mortgage at 8 percent from a previous 11 percent mortgage will save about $47,000 worth of interest over the life of a 20-year mortgage. In other words, it represents a saving of almost $200 per month.

Grandparents can also use their homes to assist in college expenses by a similar type of mortgage—a reverse annuity mortgage. While not yet available in every state, the reverse mortgage allows for a monthly payment from the bank. The mortgage and monthly payments are tied to an annuity table: The owner keeps the house until his or her death, whereupon it reverts to the bank. Like the home equity loan, it is not inexpensive to set up, and the actual interest rate may be considerable. But it can provide supplemental income and, if extra funds are available, assistance to a granddaughter or grandson in school.

Margin Accounts

One of the best loan sources is an investment banking or brokerage house. There are two major benefits from borrowing against your portfolio of securities. The first benefit is that there are no loan papers, eligibility or needs test, or credit checks. This confidential arrangement is solely between you and your broker. You can borrow, under present margin-lending requirements, up to 50 percent of the value of the portfolio. The second benefit is that interest rates are tied to the brokers' call money rate, which is the rate of interest brokers pay banks to borrow funds. This is listed in the daily business press. The broker in turn charges 1 or 2 percent above that rate, depending on the size of the account, but margin borrowing is generally cheaper than most other forms of borrowing.

You can repay the loan and eliminate the margin lending at any time you choose, and there is no prepayment penalty. There is one major danger to this type of borrowing. If the underlying securities are very volatile, the possibility exists that you may receive a margin call, which is a request for more funds. If the funds are not provided, the broker will be forced to sell some of the securities to cover the margin call. Should security prices fall drastically, by one-third from their purchase price when margin is 50 percent, they become subject to a margin call. However, if the portfolio is a reasonably conservative one, the likelihood of such a call is remote.

HIGHER EDUCATION AMENDMENTS OF 1992

After all grants have been given, work-study programs applied for and accepted, and scholarships awarded (or denied), there is still likely to be a gap between the college tuition bill and immediate family resources. Loans now play a substantial role in bridging that gap. The current average student borrower at a private college graduates with a debt of more than $10,000. That fact should be motive enough to search out the best loans, the ones with the lowest interest rates, the most flexible terms, and the longest repayment schedules.

Remember, in the mid-seventies loans made up 25 percent of a student's financial assistance. Today loans make up approximately 47 percent of such aid. That figure is likely to rise even further since costs are continuing to rise and the federal government has legislated approval for higher loan levels. As with Parkinson's law, which stipulates that people will spend up to the limit of their income, students and families are likely to borrow to the limit of their borrowing capacities.

Some of the more important regulations for loans are:

- All students applying for loans (not just those whose family incomes are greater than $30,000) must pass a needs test.

- The ceiling on cumulative undergraduate guaranteed student loans has been raised to $17,250, up from $12,500.

- The ceiling on cumulative guaranteed student loans for undergraduate and graduate work has been raised to $73,000.

Student aid is constantly being revised, rather like annual tax changes. It has not quite achieved the status of an entitlement, such as Social Security or Medicaid, and is subject to some political pressures. Happily, the pressure in the Congress has been to expand assistance in the face of domestic educational slippage and foreign competition.

The Higher Education Amendments for 1992 increased authorized maximums for some programs for another five years—though actual availability in any given year depends on whether or not the Congress appropriates the additional funds. The Pell grant maximum, for example, was increased from $2,400 to $3,700. However, whether there will be annual budget appropriations to meet that lofty goal is at the moment doubtful. In addition, eligibility was expanded by raising the family income maximum from $30,000 to $42,000. This increase has made an additional 600,000 students eligible to receive Pell grants. Moreover, the legislation authorized an increase in guaranteed student loans from $13.4 billion to $18 billion, enabling an additional one million students to participate in loan programs.

Finally, the government recently put in place regulations that will enable borrowers to repay their student loans on a 30-year schedule. This is being promoted as an aid to graduates who do not make high salaries. But it is something of a Trojan horse since the interest costs will make a college education even more expensive. A $10,000 student loan at 8 percent for five years will cost $2,165 in interest: the monthly payment will be $203. But a $10,000 loan at 8 percent for 30 years will cost $16,416 in interest: the monthly payment will be $73. Clearly, a 30-year loan should be used only as a last resort.

COLLEGE LOAN AND TUITION PROGRAMS

Increasingly, colleges are developing their own loan and tuition programs, which either take the place of government guaranteed loans or supplement them. There is quite a bit of diversity among these programs, so applicants should request full particulars from the colleges they are considering. Many of these programs are new, and some have limited resources that are available on a first come, first served basis.

Loan Programs

Tuition assistance comes in a variety of forms. A number of colleges are now in the lending business, offering loans to students and parents. Funds for these loans either come from the school or a state agency, or the loans are made in conjunction with a local or regional bank.

Loans from colleges may fall into a number of categories: Some are interest free; some are low-interest or below market rate; still others are at normal market rates. Interest-free loans are clearly the most advantageous, but these are rare and usually associated only with colleges that have large endowments. A few colleges go even further: For a select number of students who exhibit exemplary scholarship, they will forgive part or all of the loan. Below-market loans are usually derived from a school's ability to borrow from a state agency that has accumulated funds from issuing tax-exempt bonds. Most states offer such loan programs.

One example of a state-subsidized loan program is the Connecticut Higher Education Supplemental Loan Authority, which provides funds to colleges in the state for family-education loans. Thus colleges are able to make loans for a moderate interest rate of 9.75 percent per annum. Loans are available in annual amounts of $2,000 to $5,000. The loans are to the parents, not the students, and parents must be creditworthy. Indeed, they may have adjusted gross incomes up to $90,000 and still qualify. Typical loan schedules are:

Annual amount	No. of payments	Monthly payment	Total payments
$2,000	96	$29.49	$2,831.04
3,000	96	44.23	4,246.08
4,000	96	58.98	5,662.08
5,000	96	73.72	7,077.12

Many states—Massachusetts, Illinois, New Hampshire, and Pennsylvania, among others—have adopted such programs in order to encourage moderate lending practices. But the funds for these loans are usually limited, so often it is a matter of first come, first served for state-subsidized loans.

A number of quasi-official agencies or organizations have begun to offer direct loans to students. Thirty or so Ivy League colleges and other private institutions have banded together to form the Consortium on Financing Higher Education to develop a common loan program known as *Share.* In addition, a loan program known as *Excel* provides loans that may be used at any accredited degree-granting college nationwide. Funds are provided by a nonprofit New England financial group, Nellie Mae (The New England Education Loan Marketing Association). Parents must pass a credit check. What makes these loans particularly appealing to some borrowers is that they may be paid back in up to 20 years, compared to other loan schedules that require repayment in 5 or 10 years. For a list of participants and further details, call 800-EDU-LOAN, or write to Nellie Mae Inc., 50 Braintree Hill Park, Suite 300, Braintree, Massachusetts 02184-1763.

Sallie Mae (Student Loan Marketing Association) is a government-sponsored private corporation (listed on the New York Stock Exchange) that offers direct loans to parents and graduate students to finance education in the professional fields. It bases its lending rates on three-month Treasury bills and charges 3.5 percent above that key government borrowing rate. For further information, call 800-292-6868, or write to Student Loan Marketing Association, 1050 Thomas Jefferson Street, NW, Washington, D.C. 20007.

CollegeCredit, an education loan program, is sponsored by the College Board in partnership with TIAA-CREF (Teachers Insurance & Annuity Association–College Retirement Equity Fund), and Sallie Mae. The program offers an array of educational financing options for students and parents. The focus of *CollegeCredit* is not on how much a student is eligible to borrow, but on whether, and how much, a student needs to borrow. It is a single source of credit for all the major loan programs: Federal Stafford, PLUS (Parent Loans), and ExtraCredit Loans (private signature loans serviced by Knight Tuition Payment Plans, 800-879-9390). Since *CollegeCredit* is not profit driven, it provides impartial advice. And unlike other loan programs, it does not solicit—it works solely through the financial aid officer of the college.

Some individual colleges also sponsor loan programs. Market-rate loans are made by local banks, but the guarantor is the college rather than the federal government. The chief concern for the borrower should be the rate of interest to be paid, not who guarantees the loan. However, unlike the guaranteed government loans discussed in a later section (Federal Stafford Loans, Parent Loans for Undergraduate Students), these loans may require credit checks. In other words, lending banks may restrict their loans to what they consider to be creditworthy families. Resource-poor families will have to rely on government-guaranteed loans.

It bears repeating that interest charges on these college-sponsored loans, as with government-guaranteed loans, are no longer tax-deductible items for personal tax purposes. Only by using a mortgage loan or home equity loan can such carrying charges become deductible items. Thus, for tax purposes, renters of homes or apartments are at a disadvantage with regard to the deductibility of interest costs for college and postgraduate educational expenses.

Tuition Plans

In addition to straight loans, some colleges and states are developing new ways to finance a college education as costs go up and the ability to pay remains static or shrinks. One of the most popular recent innovations is prepayment of tuition by prospective applicants' families. By agreeing to pay full tuition costs now for an education in 5, 10, or 15 years, parents can lock in today's rates. Some colleges will even lend the parents the money if they are short of funds. For the parent-consumer there are a number of questions to be asked before agreeing to such a contract. Whether one's sons or daughters will want to go to that particular college is a paramount concern. There is no way of knowing years in advance. Nor is there any way of knowing whether the college will remain equally desirable in a decade or so. Moreover, prepayment is no guarantee of admission. What are the arrangements should the child wish to go elsewhere? Is all the tuition prepayment returned? How much of the accumulated interest, if any, is rebated? Might the funds be better employed in one's own investment portfolio? In short, what are the opportunity costs— how much would be earned if the funds were otherwise employed?

There are no easy answers to these questions. If school tuition keeps rising 6 to 7 percent annually, as it has in recent years, a nontaxable investment or annuity would have to equal or exceed that rate to be competitive. For someone in the 28 percent tax bracket, a taxable investment would have to have a return of 9.72

percent to equal a 7 percent increase, and an 8.24 percent return for those in the 15 percent bracket. That naturally presumes that the investment funds are already saved.

If one has to borrow at 10 percent to pay tuition that may increase by 6 percent, the exercise is not worthwhile. What would make it even less worthwhile, whether one had the funds or had to borrow them, is the real possibility that educational costs may level off. Any parent considering prepaying tuition must consider all these variables and then compare the particular program with other investment possibilities. Alumni may well feel that such a tuition program is a bargain, but other parents must use a sharp pencil to assure themselves that such prepayment programs are advantageous.

Recently a variation on tuition prepayment programs has attracted some attention. This type of plan is referred to as tuition futures, but the term is somewhat misleading. Tuition-futures programs have more in common with the bond market than with the volatile commodity markets where futures contracts are traded. They do indeed lock in a price for a product to be delivered in the future, but it is done in a conservative fashion. The colleges offering this plan actually buy zero-coupon bonds, deeply discounted federal bonds, scheduled to mature when the student starts school. For example, $19,500 of zero-coupon bonds (50 at $390 each) might be purchased when prevailing interest rates are 6.43 percent. They will be worth $50,000 in 14 years (see table of Present Value Percent on page 126).

Other institutions do not require prepayment to freeze tuition bills. They guarantee that tuition will not rise for new freshmen if a one-time premium is paid. This premium may be a flat fee or a percentage of current tuition—say 3 percent.

While other states are considering tuition plans, some already have them in place. (The steep rise in costs to administer these plans, as well as questions as to whether they are subsidizing affluent families, has created doubts about the future of such tuition plans that are already operational.) The Michigan and Florida plans are perhaps the two most popular ones.

For example, in Florida the state-backed program has sold 150,000 contracts since it was initiated in 1988. The tuition plan covers about 44 percent of all college cost for the state's nine public universities and 28 community colleges. Dormitory contracts, a major college expense, are optional.

Florida residents, age one through 17, are eligible for one of three prepaid tuition plans: the Community College Plan (60 credit hours); the University Plan (120 credit hours); and 2 + 2 Plan (2 years of community college and 2 years of university tuition).

The University Plan has three payment options, as do the other two plans. There is a single payment: for a newborn in 1994 it was $5,639; for a ten-year-old in fifth grade a single payment was $5,793. A monthly payment plan is offered: for a newborn it was $47 per month through the October of the senior year in high school; for the ten-year-old it was $84 per month. Finally, the state offers a 5-year or 55-month installment plan: for a newborn it was $121 per month; for the ten-year-old it was $124 per month.

Tuition Bonds

A number of states have followed Illinois's and North Carolina's lead by issuing municipal bonds for the purpose of financing college tuition. These securities, termed baccalaureate bonds or college savings bonds, are a form of zero-coupon bonds. They can be purchased individually by state citizens, in any amount, without belonging to any formal tuition plan.

These zero-coupon bonds are issued at a deep discount from face value (as previously noted in Chapter 3). In other words, the $5,000 bond that will mature in 10 years might be purchased for $2,750. This will provide a 5.95 percent yield to maturity—the bonds pay no annual interest, but increase in value by nearly 6 percent per year. As a form of municipal bond, they are tax free at both the federal and state levels. Thus anyone in the 15 percent tax bracket is receiving an equivalent of a pre-tax yield of 7 percent, and someone in the 28 percent bracket is getting a pre-tax yield of 8.26 percent.

There are a number of advantages to these college savings bonds:

- they can be bought with maturities ranging from 1 to 20 years

- they can be purchased whenever funds become available, such as monies from bonuses, gifts, inheritances, etc.

- they can be purchased in small lots over the years, though it is best to buy them when they are first offered

- they are tax free

- there are no penalties for early sale or for using the funds for non-educational purposes

As with most financial transactions, there are trade-offs. The disadvantages to college savings bonds are:

- they return at maturity the face value of the investment— no more

- the value of the bonds will fluctuate (more than ordinary bonds that pay interest), which may force you to take a loss or less of a profit if you are obliged to sell before maturity

- they may not cover the cost of college tuition should educational costs rise faster than anticipated

Nevertheless, baccalaureate bonds are an excellent way to save for a college education since state bonds are relatively risk free as well as tax free. You maintain control over your funds and can use them in an emergency for other purposes. Moreover, some states pay a small bonus if the bonds are indeed used to pay tuition for in-state institutions. While long-term fixed-interest investments do not generally keep up with inflation, such as in the 1980s, they should keep abreast of rising costs if the 1990s continue to be a period of low inflation.

Federal Stafford Loans

Once called the Guaranteed Student Loan, the Stafford permits students to borrow funds for educational expenses from private sources such as banks, credit unions, savings and loan associations, and educational organizations. Since Stafford loans are subsidized by the government, interest rates are lower than commercial loans. The interest rate is now variable, based on the 91-day Treasury bill rate, plus 3.1 percent, capped at 9 percent.

Repayment on both interest and principal is deferred until a student graduates or leaves school: repayment usually commences six months after departing from college.

In order to qualify, students must attend full time (except in a few states that will accommodate half-time students). The student must be a U.S. citizen or a permanent resident alien. Freshmen may borrow up to $2,625 a year, and upperclassmen may borrow larger amounts annually for a maximum of $23,000.

Graduate and professional students are eligible to borrow a maximum $65,000 including any undergraduate loans. These are subsidized loans and guaranteed by the federal government regardless of who actually issues them. There is a 5 percent origination fee, plus the possibility of a 3 percent insurance premium, depending upon the actual lender's policies.

The Higher Education Act of 1992 also created a new unsubsidized loan facility for students who do not qualify for the Stafford (cannot prove demonstrated need within terms of the guidelines) and/or who need additional assistance. While the terms of the loans are similar to the subsidized loans, interest charges begin immediately instead of when the student leaves school, though repayment can be postponed until graduation. The origination/insurance fee is 6.5 percent.

The eligibility methodology requires that an applicant for a subsidized Stafford first apply for a Pell grant. The applicant for an unsubsidized Stafford must first apply not only for a Pell grant, but also for the subsidized Stafford before being eligible for unsubsidized status.

Loans for Parents

There are two loan programs for parents to assist their children. The Federal Parent Loan for Undergraduate Students (PLUS) is a government-sponsored program for parents of dependent students: no financial-need test is required, nor are the applicants obliged to show suitable collateral. There is no restriction as to the loan's use (tuition, room and board, living expenses, etc.), and some parents use the loan to pay down the parents' contribution as computed in the need analysis. Parents may borrow up to the full cost of education less any financial aid the child has already received. The interest rate is variable, set at 3.1 percent over the one-year Treasury bill rate, with a cap of 10 percent. The loan must be repaid within 10 years, but may be refinanced and consolidated.

The ExtraCredit Loan is a privately sponsored loan for creditworthy borrowers who need more help than is available through financial aid programs and government-sponsored loan programs like PLUS. These are signature loans: no need to demonstrate financial need or collateral, but a credit check is required to prove good credit. The interest rate is set quarterly at 4.5 percent above the three-month Treasury bill rate.

Federal Perkins Loan Program

Finally, there are direct student loans administered by local colleges. The program gives priority to students with exceptional need. In order to apply, the forms are obtained from the financial aid officer of the school, not from the bank. The forms are essentially those for the Pell grant and for the Supplemental Educational Opportunity Grant (SEOG). One must be enrolled at least half time to be eligible. The actual amount of the loan is determined by the college, within federally set limits, but the cumulative limits are $4,500 during the first two years of undergraduate work, $9,000 for those who have completed two years of study, and $18,000 for graduate students (including undergraduate loans). The student's family must pass a needs test. This is the cheapest of all federally sponsored loans; there is no interest charge during school and for nine months afterwards. As noted, these loans have the lowest interest rate—set at a fixed 5 percent. These loans can sometimes be deferred up to three years for service in the military, the Peace Corps, or approved comparable organizations, or if study is resumed on at least a half-time basis.

Federal Direct Student Loan Program

The latest twist in this maze of loan programs was established late in 1993 when the Congress authorized the Department of Education to make loans to students directly, cutting out middlemen, the lenders and guarantor agencies. This is an attempt to both simplify the loan process, as well as reduce costs to the taxpayer. Whether it will save the advertised $4.3 billion during the next five-year trial period is dubious. However, there will be an attempt in this program to tailor repayment schedules to fit individual needs rather than a fixed repayment schedule. It is too soon to know if that will indeed be the case, but it is worth keeping the promise in mind.

The Federal Direct Student Loan Program is just commencing, and only 105 colleges are initial participants. Nevertheless, 300,000 students are now eligible for this program. The first benefit will be found in origination fees: they are to be fixed at a maximum of 4 percent, which is far better than the 8 percent presently found in some of the other loan programs. Clearly, it pays to inquire whether your intended school is a participant in this program.

In addition to this new program, the federal government has started a pilot program of national service. This too should be investigated for its potential benefit to some students. The core idea is to forgive $5,000 of student loans if the graduate will work for a year in national service, such as in schools, national parks, auxiliary police and other public service sectors. In return, the participant will receive approximately a $9,000 stipend.

Whether this is a desirable trade-off is problematic. Since the average college student may start work at a far higher salary, there is a very real opportunity cost to this program. A new job at $25,000 compared to a $9,000 minimum wage job, plus $5,000 forgiveness, still leaves an $11,000 negative cash flow to the participant of the national service program. Nevertheless, it is something to consider for students who may be delaying their entry into the workforce or for other personal reasons.

Miscellaneous Loan Sources

Every state has some agency or department that administers the state's programs for higher education. For example, in New York it is the Higher Education Services Corporation. These agencies will list and provide free information on all the special loans available within the state, such as loans to veterans or health-profession students. These programs are worth checking since they just may fit your special niche.

9

TAILORING FINANCIAL STRATEGIES TO PERSONAL CIRCUMSTANCES

One size fits all is okay for stretch socks, but a poor approach for college financial planning. Indeed, no two families' circumstances are identical, and in the last instance one must make personal decisions and choices. In order to help, the following are a number of scenarios for successfully meeting college costs. These case studies can, of course, be mixed and matched; they also should be reviewed periodically and revised, if necessary, as the economic weather changes.

Over any long period of saving and investing, one will be passing through customary stages of business cycles. Of late, these cycles have run between three and five years in duration. Such a cycle will encompass not only expansions and recessions, but inflations, disinflations, and deflations, high interest rates and

113

high inflation levels, followed by low interest rates and low inflation. It is not easy to catch the swings, but successful savers and investors will certainly try.

The 1990s are certainly different from the previous decade— a notion that must be fully appreciated by savers and investors. Low interest rates and a difficult investment environment certainly make the task of paying college costs more onerous. As usual, new savings and investment techniques should be met with some skepticism, and concerns about safety dictate that your money should be placed only in time-tested instruments and organizations. Diversification in both what you select and when you select it is still key to money management in the 1990s.

Part of the value of a plan is that one does not hop, skip, and jump from one savings or investment vehicle to another. At the same time, there are few, very few, dictates in the financial world that are written in stone. There are times in the course of a business cycle when it becomes prudent to switch from one form of asset to another. Thus it is reasonable to be flexible and open to change while you target your opportunities. As you read the following case studies, let them suggest alternatives and goals to apply to your own personal situation. Tax and estate considerations naturally differ and will affect each profile in varied ways. The following are meant only as general guides, not specific advice.

PROFILE 1: YOUNG FAMILY

The Background

Alice and Bobby were newlyweds, so enamored of children that they started to have them while little more than children themselves. They married right after high school and immediately started to raise a family on their new farm. Alice and Bobby have used the services of the local agricultural extension division of the state university to plan their crop plantings, to improve their livestock, and to keep up with the latest trends in farming. They have decided that their three children should attend the state university when they reach college age.

The Problem

Their children are now two, four, and five years of age. Farming income is notoriously erratic, and the last few years have been disastrous. However, they have saved some funds—$35,000— from the good years, which are on deposit with the state-insured savings and loan association (S&L) in the form of certificates of deposit. The CDs are of short maturity, and consequently of low yield, since Alice and Bobby feel they may have to use those funds if they have another bad year. The problem is how to keep reasonably liquid, build capital for their children's schooling, and save some funds for their own retirement.

The Solution

They should remove the funds from the state-insured S&L when the CDs come due. There is no point in keeping money in depositories with dubious state insurance in view of their poor regulatory record and the weak financial condition of almost a third of all thrifts. With the proceeds, Alice and Bobby might deposit

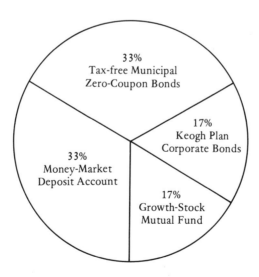

Profile 1 Solution

$10,000 in an FDIC-insured money-market deposit account. This will give them liquid money-market rates without the penalization provision of the CDs. They can add funds to this account as their income and expenses permit, and draw from it as needed.

With $11,000+, they might buy tax-free municipal zero-coupon bonds, or the equivalent special zero college bonds that some states offer. For the 5-year-old, they can purchase zeros due in 13 years, when the child is 18 years of age. A purchase of $4,100 with a yield to maturity of 7 percent will increase to $10,000 in 13 years. For the 4-year-old, $10,000 of zeros due in 14 years will cost $3,800 with a yield to maturity of 7 percent. For the 2-year-old, $10,000 of zeros due in 16 years will cost $3,333 with a yield to maturity of 7 percent.

If Alice and Bobby can repeat a similar purchase the following year, plus two subsequent years, they will have close to $40,000 for each child when ready to start college. Even if they are unable to make a comparable investment the following year, by investing smaller amounts with successively shorter maturity dates over a number of years they can accumulate substantial funds with a locked-in yield to maturity. And perhaps succeeding purchases will be at higher yields.

Finally, for their own retirement, they might split the balance of nearly $14,000 in half: some into a tax-deferred Keogh account invested in corporate bonds, some into a growth-stock mutual fund.

PROFILE 2: DIVORCED MOTHER

The Background

After her divorce and relocation, Carol finds herself in what might be called a marginal position: She is no longer an affluent suburban homemaker, but she is not destitute either. Her $40,000 lump-sum divorce settlement doesn't provide enough income to live on, so she has resumed her teaching career and earns a salary of $21,500. Child support payments for her 8-year-old daughter, Diana, increase her annual income by a few thousand dollars, but that money cannot be counted on.

The Problem

Her former husband is starting a new family, and there is little expectation that he will or can substantially assist with college expenses. How can Carol use the money she has to assure Diana's college education in 10 years?

The Solution

Though 10 years seems a long time away, Carol decides to do an informal need analysis to see how much financial aid Diana can expect and what Carol's parental contribution might be. While much may change in a decade, the exercise gives her a rough idea of what college will cost and what her financial planning goals should be. She anticipates that pay increases will bring her salary to $32,000 by the time Diana starts college, and estimates that she will be expected to contribute $7,500 toward college costs of $16,000 per year. She considers certificates of deposit, but the rates are so low that after taxes there is a negative yield. Is it possible to get a higher yield with almost equal safety?

A friend suggests that instead of buying the certificates of

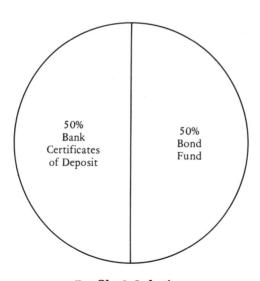

Profile 2 Solution

deposit of a local bank with a 3 or 4 percent return, she consider buying the preferred stock of a major money center bank—many of which are yielding 8 or 9 percent. While the preferred stock is not guaranteed by the FDIC, she believes that the bank crisis at the end of the 1980s is over. The difference in rates alone is worth half a year of college costs.

With the balance, she invests in a closed-end global bond fund where the rates are about 8 percent. Since these funds contain both U.S. Treasury bonds and bonds of other governments, she feels reasonably secure, though she knows that the principal will fluctuate inversely to interest rates.

PROFILE 3: YOUNG PROFESSIONALS, TWO INCOMES

The Background

Frank and Gloria are young professionals on the fast track—he is a radiologist and she is a pharmacist. Their combined earnings place them in the top tax bracket. They have one daughter, Helen, but may have more children in the future. Income is no issue, but holding on to their ample cash flow is proving to be a problem now, and will become a bigger one when Gloria stops work to have more children. They have just received a $25,000 inheritance.

The Problem

Though both are professionals, they are still W-2 people: All their active income is attributable to their jobs. How can they reduce income taxes while accumulating capital? Can they save for their children's education without unduly benefiting the tax collector? What should they do with the windfall inheritance?

The Solution

Through monthly deposits of $700 in a money-market mutual fund over the past five years, Frank and Gloria have jointly saved

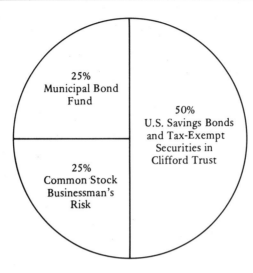

Profile 3 Solution

$50,000 of capital that is now throwing off substantial interest, though at a much lower rate than when they started. In addition, they have $25,000 in a Super-NOW checking account now paying about 2.5 percent. The current earnings from both accounts are fully taxed. Their real return after inflation and taxes is decidedly negative.

They consider setting up a short-term, or Clifford, trust for their children to give $50,000 to the trust. However, the pre-1986 tax advantage was to shift earned income to the children through the trust—a provision that was subsequently repealed. Today, short-term trusts will be taxed at the rates of their grantors, not their beneficiaries. On reflection, Frank and Gloria realize that these rates are immaterial since they decide to emphasize growth rather than income—and save the costs of setting up and administering such a trust. Therefore, the $50,000 is invested in aggressive growth funds that pay no dividends.

Another $25,000 is transferred from the Super-NOW account and placed in a municipal bond fund to increase their tax-free income. Finally, their inheritance, representing another quarter of their family assets, might be placed in common stocks designated for growth and income.

PROFILE 4: WIDOWED FATHER, INDEPENDENT BUSINESSMAN

The Background

Ike owns a small electronics research and development company. His wife died and he is now the sole support of three children. Business has been good to him and he has amassed savings and investment assets of $250,000.

The Problem

Up to now Ike has concentrated exclusively on his work and business, but as his oldest son, John, is reaching college age, he realizes that he has all but neglected to plan for college costs. He must now move quickly in planning for John and the two other boys, who are 16 and 14 years old.

The Solution

He decides to give each son a 10 percent share of the business. On the $125,000 of annual profit, the sons are then entitled to $12,500 each. This effectively lowers the father's tax bite while improving the incomes of his sons for a nominal tax consequence. Since the father was in the 28 percent tax bracket, divesting through these gifts actually saves him some $10,000 in personal taxes. The sons are each taxed on the $12,500, about $1,100 after deductions and exemptions, a net saving to the family of over $7,000. While there may be some initial gift tax to the father, depending on the value of the company's shares, he has successfully shifted income to the children to take advantage of their lower tax brackets. With his assets, Ike has decided to set up a Crummey trust and place in it three $25,000 Ginnie Mae certificates. Perhaps he will be able to contribute more in subsequent years. Meanwhile, he retains control of the funds. These certificates will throw off one of the highest rates of interest, about one full percentage point above any other federal-guaranteed paper.

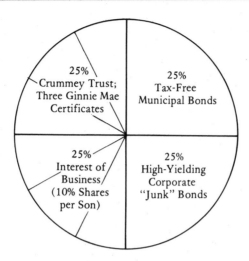

Profile 4 Solution

As the monthly income is received by the trust, it will be reinvested until each child reaches his majority. The children as beneficiaries can then either take out the income and principal or let it accumulate for educational purposes. The income not withdrawn or distributed to the children is taxed at the trust's rates. As for the balance of his assets, $175,000, Ike has divided them equally between tax-free municipals and high-yielding junk bonds.

PROFILE 5: INDEPENDENT PROFESSIONALS

The Background

Ken and Lisa have one mentally retarded child in a special-education facility and one child who is starting to apply for college. Ken is an oral surgeon and Lisa runs his office. Of late they have started to accumulate some savings after years of paying off a medical education and the costs associated with caring for a retarded child.

The Problem

How can they generate enough income to provide for the expensive medical costs of their younger child, while sending the older child to a private college and postgraduate school?

The Solution

With their $100,000 of savings and family assets, they decide that they will buy $50,000 of a Ginnie Mae mutual fund to assist in the educational program of their retarded child. Since they are in a high tax bracket, they put the fund in the child's name. This will exceed their gift-tax exclusion, but it will not be a taxable transaction under the unified credit. Ken and Lisa can give their children any amount of money for tuition or medical costs, but their earnings on their capital would be subject to a high tax rate.

For the child nearing college age, Ken and Lisa's professional corporation decides to give their small medical building to a trust (either a Clifford or a Crummey will do, but the trustee must be

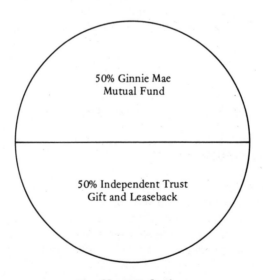

Profile 5 Solution

independent) of which the college-bound child is the beneficiary. The professional corporation and the trustee then enter into a written agreement to lease the premises back to the professional corporation. The rent, $10,000 a year, is an ordinary and necessary business expense, thus deductible from the revenues of the practice. The trust then has $10,000 of annual income to invest and/or pay for tuition costs. The income to the trust is taxable, but there may be depreciation expenses that will offset some of that taxable income.

PROFILE 6: GRANDPARENTS AND ORPHANED GRANDCHILDREN

The Background

Marty and Nora were simultaneously killed in an automobile accident, leaving behind two daughters and one son. Their life insurance was ample, $100,000, and the proceeds under the will were to be administered by Nora's parents as custodians of their grandchildren.

The Problem

How can the grandparents raise a second family, maintain their own living standard, and provide for educational costs that might be incurred after they have died?

The Solution

The grandparents thought first of establishing a Minor trust [Section 2503 (c) trust] for the children, but on closer examination there seemed to be no real advantages. First of all, a trust is expensive to set up and maintain, with legal and accounting fees. More important, a trust does not create any tax savings (indeed trust tax rates are somewhat higher than that for unemployed children) since the insurance inheritance not only passes to the children tax free, but the funds are legally and irrevocably theirs and do not belong to the deceased parents' estate or the custodial grandparents. The grandparents set up three custodial accounts (at no cost). One-third of the insurance money—$33,333—was deposited into each child's account, plus their share of their parents' estate, another $25,000 each. As custodians, the grandparents can deposit money, manage investments, and distribute principal and income to pay all bills. Since the children are orphans, there is no question of any expenses being disallowed, that is, the income being taxed to the grandparents as obligatory supports. The custodianship must cease when the children reach their majorities, and all interest and principal must be distributed to them.

The grandparents decide that half of their accounts should be used for present maintenance and half should be saved for higher educational costs. With one-half of each child's account invested for current income, they take half of the $58,333, $29,167: They buy $14,500 of municipal bonds for tax-free income and $14,500 of a Ginnie Mae fund. With the other $29,167 they buy equal shares of United States savings bonds (EE series) and a mutual fund of blue-chip stocks. The current income portion will give the children a safe and reasonably high yield without a heavy tax bill, while the educational savings will provide at least a 6 percent

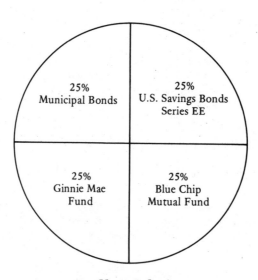

Profile 6 Solution

return (perhaps more if rates are adjusted upward) on the savings bonds and a chance to increase the portfolio's rate of return by purchasing quality corporate stock.

Factors to Keep in Mind

No matter which of the preceding scenarios is relevant to your situation, and no matter which configuration of savings and investment vehicles you ultimately use, there are some general financial techniques worth considering in the quest for college funding.

- Savings are subject to the ravages of inflation and taxation. This combination makes the act of saving money a Sisyphean task, like trying to make headway on a treadmill. The only way to gain ground is to save at the highest rate of interest, at the lowest level of taxation, with the added fillip of an investment that significantly increases your overall rate of return.

- Saving for college is easiest (or, perhaps, least painful) when begun early. Money takes a long time to double when saving at fixed rates of interest—nine years when the interest rate is 8 percent.

- Whether money should be saved in the name of the parents or the child is a debatable subject. For affluent families with substantial incomes, six figures of net worth, and only one or two children to educate, the chances for significant financial aid are not great. Consequently, it is better to save in the children's names or in a trust, especially after they reach age 14, to take advantage of children's preferential tax treatment. For less affluent families with several college-bound youngsters, the expectations of financial aid are greater. In the latter case, it is perhaps better to save in the parents' names.

- Children can receive a gift of up to $10,000 per year per parent without any tax consequences to donor or donee.

- Trust income is taxed at a slightly higher rate than a child's income.

- Savings rates or interest rates are determined by a yield curve in the money markets. Under normal conditions, the short maturities obtain less interest than medium- or long-term maturities. When possible, money should be lent on a long-term basis for the greatest yield. Maturity dates, however, should be spread out so that diversity offers protection against short-term adverse interest-rate movements.

- Zero-coupon bonds of the United States Treasury, zero municipal bonds, and compound-interest bonds of corporations have all earned themselves a place in long-term savings plans—whether for college funding, retirement benefits, or just plain savings. Since their introduction in the early eighties, their popularity has grown enormously.

- In order to calculate the present value of these deeply discounted obligations, the following table contains factors which, when multiplied by the investment goal, reveal what must be invested initially to attain that figure. If you wished to reach $50,000 in 14 years, and you could purchase a 9 percent compounding rate debt instrument, you multiply $50,000 by 29.221 percent: $14,611 of these bonds must be purchased. In other words, you will need 50 bonds that currently sell at $292.21 to reach your objective.

Present Value Percent

Years to maturity	7.00%	8.00%	8.50%	9.00%	9.50%
10	50.257	45.778	43.589	41.555	39.529
12	43.800	39.088	36.904	34.846	32.832
14	38.170	33.413	31.244	29.221	27.270
16	33.260	28.561	26.452	24.503	22.650
18	28.980	24.414	22.395	20.547	18.812
20	25.260	20.869	18.961	17.230	15.625

APPENDIX A

1994 TAX RATE SCHEDULES

The 1986 Tax Reform Act replaced the 14-bracket rate structure, which had rates ranging from 11 to 50 percent. Now there are five brackets: 15, 28, 31, 36, and 39.6%.

Single—Schedule X

If line 5 is: Over—	But not over—	The tax is:	of the amount over—
$0	$22,750	..........15%	$0
22,750	55,100	$3,412.50 + 28%	22,750
55,100	115,000	12,470.50 + 31%	55,100
115,000	250,000	31,039.50 + 36%	115,000
250,000	....	79,639.50 + 39.6%	250,000

Married Filing Jointly or Qualifying Widow(er)—Schedule Y-1

If line 5 is: Over—	But not over—	The tax is:	of the amount over—
$0	$38,000	..........15%	$0
38,000	91,850	$5,700.00 + 28%	38,000
91,850	140,000	20,778.00 + 31%	91,850
140,000	250,000	35,704.50 + 36%	140,000
250,000	....	75,304.50 + 39.6%	250,000

127

Head of Household—Schedule Z

If line 5 is: Over—	But not over—	The tax is:	of the amount over—
$0	$30,500	..........15%	$0
30,500	78,700	$4,575.00 + 28%	30,500
78,700	127,500	18,071.00 + 31%	78,700
127,500	250,000	33,199.00 + 36%	127,500
250,000	....	77,299.00 + 39.6%	250,000

Married Filing Separately—Schedule Y-2

If line 5 is: Over—	But not over—	The tax is:	of the amount over—
$0	$19,000	.........15%	$0
19,000	45,925	$2,850.00 + 28%	19,000
45,925	70,000	10,389.00 + 31%	45,925
70,000	125,000	17,852.25 + 36%	70,000
125,000	....	37,652.25 + 39.6%	125,000

APPENDIX B

GIFT TAX TABLE

Unified Rate Schedule

Taxable amount equal to or more than— (1)	Taxable amount less than— (2)	Tax on amount in column (1) (3)	Rate of tax on excess over amount in column (1) (4)
0	10,000	0	18%
10,000	20,000	1,800	20
20,000	40,000	3,800	22
40,000	60,000	8,200	24
60,000	80,000	13,000	26
80,000	100,000	18,200	28
100,000	150,000	23,800	30
150,000	250,000	38,800	32
250,000	500,000	70,800	34
500,000	750,000	155,800	37
750,000	1,000,000	248,300	39
1,000,000	1,250,000	345,800	41
1,250,000	1,500,000	448,300	43
1,500,000	2,000,000	555,800	45
2,000,000	2,500,000	780,800	49

Source: IRS Publication 904, *Interrelated Computations for Estate and Gift Taxes.*

129

APPENDIX C

INCOME TAX RATE SCHEDULE FOR TRUSTS

The income tax schedule for estates and trusts is as follows:

In 1994, if taxable income is:	The tax is:
Not over $5,000	15% of taxable income
Over $5,000	28% of taxable income

APPENDIX D

INTEREST RATES AND YIELDS

Interest rates are certainly a key to profitable saving, but they are not simple to calculate without tables or a calculator or computer. Here are a few facts to clarify the subject:

- The federal consumer Truth-in-Lending law requires that interest rates on consumer loans be stated in annual percentage rate (APR) terms.

- The formula for simple interest is *Interest* = *Principal* × *Rate* of Interest × *Time* or $I = P \times R \times T$. On simple interest, the borrower has to pay interest *only* on the amount borrowed and *not* on any accumulated interest charges.

- Compound interest is the amount paid or earned on the original principal *plus* the accumulated interest. With interest compounding, the more periods for which interest is calculated, the more rapidly the amount of interest on interest *and* interest on principal builds. Compounding annually means that there is only one period annually when interest is calculated. The formula for compound interest is: $F = P (1 + R)^T$, in which F is the total future repayment value of a loan (principal *plus* the total accumulated or compound interest), P is the principal, R is the rate of interest per year or annual percentage rate, and T is the time in years.

131

- The difference between the advertised interest rate and the actual yield offered by depository institutions is a function of compounding. The more frequently the bank compounds, the higher the actual interest rate. A $10,000 deposit at 5 percent will earn $500 if it is compounded annually. The interest rate and the yield are the same. If the sum is compounded quarterly, every three months, at the end of the year it will have earned $509 at 5 percent, a yield of 5.09 percent. If the sum is compounded daily, at the end of the year it will have earned $513 at 5 percent, a yield of 5.13 percent.

- Money doubles: the rule of 72. In order to calculate how long it will take to double your money at a given interest rate, the formula is:

$$\frac{72}{\text{interest rate}} = \text{years to double}$$

Interest rate	Years
2.0	36.00
4.0	18.00
6.0	12.00
7.0	10.29
9.0	8.00
11.0	6.55

APPENDIX E

WORKSHEETS AND TABLES

You may find the following worksheets and tables (based on the Federal Methodology) helpful in completing your own need analysis estimate. You may use Column B for that purpose. The worksheets were completed in Column A for a hypothetical two-parent family (older parent is 50) with two incomes and one child, who is planning to attend a higher cost, private college. The worksheets include:

Worksheet 1: Estimating student expenses
Worksheet 2: Estimating parents' contribution
Worksheet 3: Student's expected contribution
Worksheet 4: Total family contribution
Worksheet 5: Estimating financial need
Worksheet 6: Financial aid awards

Worksheet 1: Estimating student expenses	Column A	Column B
1. Tuition and fees	$ 8,900	$
2. Books and supplies	250	
3. Student's room	3,300	
4. Student's board/meals*	1,100	
5. Personal (clothing, laundry, recreation, medical)	800	
6. Transportation**	650	
7. Other (such as costs of child care, extra expenses because of handicap)		
A. Total budget (add 1–7)	$15,000	$

* These should be considered family expenses if student lives at home.
** If student plans to live on campus, estimate the costs of two or three round trips home during the year. If student plans to live at home, estimate costs of daily transportation to and from college.

133

Worksheet 2: Estimating parents' contribution	Column A	Column B
Previous year's income:		
1. Father's yearly wages, salaries, tips, and other compensation	$20,000	
2. Mother's yearly wages, salaries, tips, and other compensation	15,000	
3. All other income of mother and father (dividends, interest, social security, pensions, welfare, etc.). Include IRA/Keogh payments and 401 (k) and 403 (b) contributions.	500	
4. Adjustments to income, such as business expenses, interest penalties, alimony paid, etc. Do not include IRA/Keogh payments.	$ 250	
B. Total income (Add 1, 2, and 3 and subtract 4)	$35,250	
Expenses:		
5. U.S. income tax parents expect to pay on their 1994 income (not amount withheld from paycheck)	3,407	
6. Social Security (FICA) tax (See Table for 6)	2,678	
7. State and other taxes (insert 8% of B)	2,820	
8. Employment allowance. If 2-parent family and both parents work, allow 35% of lower salary to a maximum of $2,500; if 1-parent family, allow 35% of salary to a maximum of $2,500. No allowance for a 2-parent family in which only one parent works.	2,500	
9. Income Protection Allowance (See Table for 9)	17,150	
C. Total allowances against income (Add 5, 6, 7, 8, 9)	$28,555	
D. Available income (Subtract C from B)	$ 6,695	

Worksheet 2: Estimating parents' contribution	Column A	Column B
Assets:		
10. Other real estate equity (equity on property other than the family home; value minus unpaid balance on mortgage)		
11. Business or farm (Figure total value minus indebtedness and then take percentage shown in Table for 11.) If your family is only part owner of the farm or business, list only your share of the net value.		
12. Cash, savings, and checking accounts	$ 2,500	
13. Other investments (current net value)	7,500	
E. Total assets (Add 10, 11, 12, 13)	$10,000	
Deductions:		
F. Asset protection allowance (See Table for F)	$44,100	
G. Remaining assets (Subtract F from E)	(34,100)	
H. Income supplement from assets (Multiply G by 12%, if negative, enter 0)	0	
I. Adjusted available income (Add D and H)	6,695	
J. Parents' expected contribution (Multiply I by taxation rate amount given in Table for J)	$ 1,473	
K. Parents' expected contribution if more than one family member is in college (Divide J by number of family members in college at least half-time)	$ 1,473	

Worksheet 3: Student's expected contribution	Column A	Column B
L. Student's 1994 income:		
14. Student's yearly wages, salaries, tips, and other compensation		
15. Spouse's yearly wages, salaries, tips, and other compensation		
16. All other income of student (dividends, interest, untaxed income, and benefits)	$1,000	
M. Total income (Add 4, 15, and 16)	1,000	
Allowances:		
17. U.S. income tax student (and spouse) paid on 1994 income (not amount withheld from paychecks)		
18. State and other taxes (enter 4% of M)		
19. Social Security (FICA) tax (See Table for 19)		
20. Dependent student offset	1,750	
N. Total allowances against student's income (Add 17, 18, 19, and 20)	1,750	
O. Available income (Subtract N from M)	(750)	
Resources:		
21. Contribution from income (Line O × 50%) cannot be less than $0	0	
22. Contribution from assets (Multiply the total savings and other assets—such as stocks and bonds excluding home equity by 35%)	350	
23. Other gifts and scholarships already received		
Q. Total student resources (Add 21, 22, and 23)	$350	

Worksheet 4: Total family contribution	Column A	Column B
J. **Parents' expected contribution** (Use figure for K instead of J if there is more than one family member in college.)	$1,473	
Q. **Student's expected contribution from resources**	350	
R. **Total family contribution** (Add J and Q)	$1,823	

Worksheet 5: Estimating financial need	Column A	Column B
S. **Total budget**	$15,000	
R. **Total family contribution**	1,823	
T. **Student need** (Subtract R from S)	$13,177	

Worksheet 6: Financial aid awards	Column A	Column B
A. **Total student budget**	$15,000	
M. **Total family contribution**	1,823	
N. **Demonstrated financial need**	13,177	
1. Federal Pell Grant	—	
2. State scholarship	2,500	
3. Institutional grant	3,000	
4. Federal Work-Study	2,502	
5. Federal Perkins	1,800	
6. Federal Stafford Loan	2,625	
7. Federal PLUS Loan	—	
8. Private scholarships	750	
Total financial aid	$13,177	

Table for Social Security (FICA) tax allowance (Items 6 and 19)

Wages	
$1 to 60,600	7.65% of income earned by each wage earner (maximum $4,636 per person)
$60,601 or more	$4,636 + 1.45% of income earned above $60,600 by each wage earner

Table for income protection allowance (Item 9)

Family size* (including student)	Number in college**				
	1	2	3	4	5
2	$11,150	$ 9,240			
3	13,890	11,990	10,080		
4	17,150	15,240	13,350	11,440	
5	20,240	18,330	16,430	14,520	12,620
6	23,670	21,760	19,860	17,960	$16,060

* For each additional family member, add $2,670
** For each additional college student, subtract $1,900

Table for adjusted net worth of a business or farm (Item 11)

Net worth (NW)	Adjusted net worth
Less than $1	$ 0
$ 1 to 80,000	0 + 40% of NW
$ 80,001 to 240,000	32,000 + 50% of NW over $ 80,000
$240,001 to 400,000	112,000 + 60% of NW over 240,000
$400,001 or more	208,000 + 100% of NW over 400,000

Table for asset protection allowance (Item F)

Age of older parent or student	Couple/married	Unmarried/single
25 or under	$ 0	$ 0
26	2,300	1,600
27	4,600	3,200
28	6,900	4,900
29	9,100	6,500
30	11,400	8,100
31	13,700	9,700
32	16,000	11,300
33	18,300	13,000
34	20,600	14,600
35	22,900	16,200
36	25,200	17,800
37	27,400	19,400
38	29,700	21,100
39	32,000	22,700
40	34,300	24,300
41	35,200	24,700
42	36,100	25,300
43	37,000	25,800
44	38,000	26,500
45	38,900	26,900
46	39,900	27,600
47	40,900	28,300
48	42,000	29,000
49	43,000	29,500
50	44,100	30,200
51	45,500	30,900
52	46,700	31,700
53	48,100	32,500
54	49,700	33,400
55	50,900	34,200
56	52,500	35,000
57	54,100	36,000
58	55,700	37,100
59	57,700	37,900
60	59,500	39,000
61	61,600	40,100
62	63,400	41,300
63	65,600	42,400
64	67,900	43,600
65 or over	70,200	45,100

Table for parents' expected contribution (Item J)	
Adjusted available income (AAI)	*Total parents' contribution*
Less than $3,409	$ 750
$ 3,409 to $10,000	22% of AAI
10,001 to 12,500	$2,200 + 25% of AAI over $10,000
12,501 to 15,100	2,825 + 29% of AAI over 12,500
15,101 to 17,600	3,579 + 34% of AAI over 15,100
17,601 to 20,100	4,429 + 40% of AAI over 17,600
20,101 or more	5,429 + 47% of AAI over 20,100

GLOSSARY

bearer form Bonds issued in bearer form belong to whomever possesses them. Thus they are easily transferable, like dollar bills, and leave no telltale tax traces. With book-entry bookkeeping, they are losing their popularity.

bond A promissory note from a corporation or government agency for the face value of a loan plus a fixed (coupon) rate of interest, usually paid twice yearly. Bonds do not represent ownership, as do stocks, but are considered a debt with an indenture administered by a trustee (usually a bank) to act as a representative of the bondholder. Upon the maturity date, the full face value of the bond is redeemed. The price of a bond will fluctuate in the secondary market as current prevailing interest rates rise and fall.

bond funds Bond funds are of two kinds: The first is rather like a stock mutual fund, composed of a variety of different issues, depending on the purposes and objectives of the fund. A junk bond fund is one composed of highly speculative, high-yielding securities. The second kind of bond fund is one that takes collateral mortgage bonds as its primary portfolio, such as a Ginnie Mae fund, which passes on to the shareholders interest and principal from the mortgages on a monthly basis. These are also called income funds.

capital Derived from the Greek word for cattle, capital is the principal invested in an asset or a business. Capital may be thought of as the amount of income left after taxes.

capital endowments Money, securities, or other assets given or bestowed on a foundation, university, or other organization to assist in covering costs.

141

capital-gains tax   A tax levied on profits realized on the sale of securities and other assets. Under the new tax code, profits from such gains are taxed as ordinary income.

certificate of deposit (CD)   Banks and thrifts issue CDs for six months to five years in duration. The longer the maturity date, the higher the interest rate. Some banks offer designer CDs, that is, they will customize the instrument, indicating what principal is necessary to arrive at a given goal. While CDs do not suffer from any interest-rate risk, they are subject to penalties if they are cashed in before their maturity date.

closed-end unit trust   Unlike an open-end mutual fund, which can continue to sell shares, the closed-end unit trust sells a fixed amount of shares to raise a required amount of capital. Shares of unit trusts are occasionally listed on the stock exchanges and can frequently be bought at a discount from their net asset value.

commercial paper   Loan instruments between companies, usually corporations of substantial standing. The loan is offered on a short-term basis, at an interest rate slightly below the lending rate of commercial banks.

consumer price index (CPI)   A measurement of living expenses by the Bureau of Labor Statistics to calculate the standard of living.

coupon rate   The coupon rate is the interest rate affixed to a bond when it is issued. The rate remains constant throughout the life of the bond and indicates how much money will be paid semi-annually.

credit union   A cooperative financial banking organization where depositors are usually members of the same fraternal organization or employees of the same company. Service charges are low since credit unions are nonprofit organizations.

debenture   A form of bond, but unlike most bonds there is no set collateral or property represented by the debenture. In short, it is a promissory note, issued on the good name of the company, pledging to pay principal and interest. It is usually ranked somewhat lower than bonds by credit-rating agencies.

deflation   The reverse effect of inflation as prices and wages fall in real terms. Deflation should not be confused with disinflation, a condition where the rise in prices is moderated.

demand deposits   An account held at a bank or thrift where funds are available whenever needed, that is, upon demand. Before deregulation, demand deposits paid no interest. Since deregulation, depositories offer NOW, Super-NOW, and special checking accounts that do offer interest.

Depository Institutions Deregulation and Monetary Control Act (DIDMCA)   (see **deregulation**)

deregulation   Deregulation of the financial world formally began in 1980 when Congress phased out interest-rate ceilings on bank accounts by passing the Depository Institutions Deregulation and Monetary Control Act. The act also eliminated state usury laws on residential mortgages.

discounted instrument   The market price of a security when it is sold or bought below its face or nominal value. A bond is at a discount when it sells below par ($1,000), and at a premium when it sells above it. Some initial public offerings of bonds are sold at deep discounts, such as zero-coupon bonds, that pay no interest. The interest takes the form of capital appreciation of the asset.

diversification   A spreading out of investments in different fields, or with a variety of companies. This helps to hedge against the volatility of markets. Diversifying or averaging with regard to time is also another way to hedge against market risk.

educational benefit trusts (EBTs)   These benefit programs are established by companies to help employees with college and postgraduate educational expenses. Such contributions are fully tax deductible to the business.

electronic fund transfers (automatic transfer service)   A computer banking system in which an account holder can conduct certain banking transactions from a home terminal or an automatic teller machine.

equities   (see **stock, common**)

estate planning   A terminal plan for the disposition of all property upon death. A detailed estate plan encompasses a will and trust agreements.

401 (k) salary-reduction plans　Salary-reduction plans allow employees to put away as much as $8,475 each year without having to pay income taxes on their contribution. The monies are taxed upon withdrawal at retirement. The funds are sometimes matched by the employer and invested by the employer or its agent. One benefit over Keoghs or IRAs: Employees can usually borrow against their accounts to meet college costs.

Garn-St Germain Depository Institutions Act　This act was passed in 1982, continuing the work of the 1980 DIDMCA (see **deregulation**) by allowing banks and savings and loan associations to establish money-market deposit accounts to compete with the money-market funds of investment companies and brokerage houses. The act also gave additional powers to the FDIC and FSLIC to aid and merge insolvent depositories across state lines and even interindustry if they saw the need for such actions.

gift tax　A tax levied by the federal government (and some states) on gifts valued at more than $10,000. This tax is to be paid by the donor, not by the recipient. The tax may be applied against the lifetime unified credit, which allows for gifts of $600,000 before the actual levy.

indexing　In economics, the use of the consumer price index to adjust the cost of living allowance in wage contracts and social-security benefits. In finance, the attempt to imitate the movement of the general averages such as the Dow Jones Industrial Average or Standard and Poor's 500.

Individual Retirement Account (IRA)　A retirement benefit program now available as a tax deduction only to individuals not covered by company pension plans. The maximum $2,000 annual contribution for a single person ($2,250 for a married person with a nonworking spouse) without a pension plan is tax deductible within certain limits. The IRA may earn interest or capital that will not be taxed until withdrawn.

inflation　Inflation occurs when the buying power of the dollar decreases and, conversely, the cost of goods and services increases. Generally, there are two types of inflation: cost–push and demand–pull. A cost–push inflation happens when costs rise because shortages push prices up. Demand–pull inflation is due to high demand and low availability due to natural or man-made circumstances. In either case, inflation is an economic response to rapid increase in the money supply.

interest-free loans   At one time interest-free loans were a form of tax avoidance. New laws now subject all loans (even between family members) to an imputed rate of interest on which taxes must be paid by the lender.

interest-rate risk   Fixed-interest securities are always subject to interest-rate risk. Should the prevailing interest rates go higher than the fixed rate, the bond will lose value. Conversely, if the interest rates drop, the bond will appreciate.

investment banking house   Financial bankers for corporations that need expertise in mergers, acquisitions, reorganization, etc., in raising equity capital for public offerings of their common stock. They also aid in underwriting bond issues for corporations and government agencies.

junk bonds   These are bonds that are rated as speculative by the rating agencies. They offer very high yields, yields that are in danger of not being covered by the company's earnings.

Keogh plan   A tax-advantaged retirement plan for nonincorporated businesses and the self-employed. The annual contribution is tax deductible, and it may compound tax free until it is withdrawn at retirement, when taxes must be paid.

liquidity   The ability to buy and sell securities on short notice, without substantial price differential. Liquidity is the hallmark of good markets, enabling easy and rapid convertibility of financial assets. Dollars are extremely liquid, whereas real estate holdings are extremely illiquid.

maturity   The date on which an investment principal becomes due or the date at which an option or contract expires.

money-market deposit account   A type of bank account initiated by banks and thrifts in 1983 as a result of deregulation. Rates of interest in these accounts fluctuate weekly or monthly and reflect the conditions of the free money markets. Such accounts are insured by the federal government, unlike those offered by money-market funds, but they do pay somewhat less than comparable funds.

money-market fund   A mutual fund comprised of high-yielding securities such as bank certificates of deposit, federal securities, banker's acceptances, and other highly liquid investments. These funds offer reliable high-yielding investments, but they are usually not insured as are money-market deposit accounts from banks.

mutual fund   An open-ended pool of money managed by an investment company to invest in securities. Shares in a mutual fund represent fractional ownership of the underlying net-asset value of the mutual fund.

National Longitudinal Study (NLS)   A long-term study of the National Center for Education Statistics of the Department of Education first started with the high school class of 1972. The study is an attempt to throw some light on educational attainment and labor-market experience. There have been four follow-up surveys so far, and more are promised.

no-call provision   Some bonds are issued with a no-call provision, which guarantees that regardless of falling interest rates, the bond issuers will not redeem the bond early in order to save interest costs.

portfolio   The financial holdings of an individual or corporation.

prime rate   The rate of interest a commercial bank charges its preferred customers on loans. Preferred customers usually include big corporations and other reliable clients.

principal   The original amount of a loan, deposit, or transaction. The principal may earn interest if it is in an interest-bearing account. The face value of a bond is also considered as the principal, earning interest on the basis of the coupon (interest) rate of the bond.

promissory note   Documentation for a debt drawn up between borrower and lender to include amount and type of debt, interest rate, payment schedule, and list of all parties involved.

registered form   Increasingly, bonds are sold in registered form, and all new municipal bond offerings must be sold in registered form. While registered securities protect the owner from loss, they also ensure compliance with revenue obligations.

rollover   The renewal of a loan agreement or a mortgage. Commonly used in moving an IRA or Keogh account from one custodian to another, or a qualified employee benefit plan to an IRA. For tax purposes, such a rollover has no tax consequences if completed within 60 days.

S corporation This is a special type of corporation whose shareholders elect to be taxed as individuals. In other words, all earnings flow through to the owners without payment of any corporation tax.

share draft Payment on request of a depositor of a credit union to pay a third party against the depositor's credit union account. Simply, a check.

stock (common) A fractional share of ownership in a company. The owner is entitled to dividends, if any are declared by the board of directors, plus the appreciation or depreciation of the equity in the marketplace.

stock (preferred) The owner of preferred stock has first claim on the earnings of a company. Preferred stock usually has a set dividend, which not only is paid before the common stock dividend but may be cumulative, thus receiving back dividends from years when they may have been omitted due to poor earnings.

tax-exempt bond Any issue of a municipality, agency, county, authority, or other body that is exempt from federal taxation. Buyers of these bond issues, called municipals ("munis"), are not obliged to pay federal, state, or local taxes in their state of residency.

time deposits Time deposits were traditionally accounts that paid interest from the day of deposit until the stipulated maturity date. Premature withdrawal or the termination of certificates of deposit may cause the bank or thrift to penalize the depositor. Since deregulation, both time and demand deposits pay interest, but the longer the depositor can commit his or her funds, the higher the rate of interest.

Treasury bills A type of debt security sold by the federal government to the general public. These are short-term investments, usually lasting between three months and one year. They are discounted, that is, sold at a discount from face value. The discount is approximately the rate of interest of the bill.

Treasury bond   A debt instrument sold to the general public by the government as a long-term security with a maturation date between 10 and 30 years.

Treasury note   The same as a Treasury bond but with a shorter maturity, ranging from 2 to 10 years.

Treasury paper   A generic term for bills, bonds, and notes issued by the federal government.

trusts   Trusts are separate, legal entities established for the benefit of someone or something. Trusts are established by a grantor or donor, for the benefit of a beneficiary, administered by a trustee, and eventually terminated when the principal in the trust is turned over to a remainderman. There are a number of different types, such as living and testamentary trusts, each with its own set of legal and tax consequences.

unified credit   The total amount allowed over a lifetime as a credit against the annual gift tax. In other words, you may use the unified credit to reduce any gift tax for which you may be liable.

yield   The amount or rate of return on an investment or property.

yield curve   The yield curve is a graphic demonstration of interest rates. An ordinary yield curve will show that short-term funds obtain a lower rate of interest than medium- or long-term funds. An inverted yield curve indicates that short-term money is demanding a higher rate of interest than long-term funds.

zero-coupon bonds   Zero-coupon bonds are issued without provision for semi-annual interest payments. They are issued at a deep discount from their face value but accumulate value as they mature. The discount is equivalent to the interest rate. While some corporations have issued zeros, most of them are either issued by the Treasury or are formed by investment banking houses, which issue receipts against Treasury bonds held by a custodian. The original Treasury issues are called STRIPS (Separate Trading of Registered Interest and Principal of Securities). The receipts are traded either as CATS (Certificates of Accrual on Treasury Receipts), which are traded on the New York Stock Exchange under bonds, or TIGRS (Treasury Investment Growth Receipts), which are traded over the counter.

INDEX

annuities, 52

baby-boom generation, 2
baccalaureate bonds, 108–9
bank accounts
  certificates of deposit, 16, 28–30
  lines of credit, 97–101
  money-market deposit, 17–18, 26–28, 32
  NOW and Super-NOW, 24–25
  passbook savings, 22–24
  under Uniform Gifts to Minors Act, 62–63
bank cards (credit cards), 97
bankers acceptances, 16
banks
  deregulation of, 14–15
  lines of credit from, 97–101
  savings accounts in, 22–24
beneficiary, 74–75
bills, Treasury, 15, 16, 35–37
blue chip stocks, 52
bonds
  baccalaureate, 108–9
  college savings, 108–9
  corporate, 43–45, 48–50
  municipal, 43–48, 71, 108–9
  Treasury, 35–37, 41–43
  U.S. savings, 32–34, 70–71
  zero-coupon, 41–45, 107–9
borrowbacks, 64–65
borrowing, 95–112

  from college loan and tuition programs, 103–12
  within family, 64–65
  Higher Education Amendments of 1992 and, 102–3
  home equity loans, 99–101
  interest-free, 64–65, 104
  from life insurance policies, 52–53, 54
  lines of credit for, 97–101
  margin accounts, 101–2
  from retirement plans, 90–94
  see also loans
brokers, 51
  margin accounts with, 101–2
business cycles, 2
businesses
  borrowing from retirement plans of, 90–94
  children as partners in, 85–87
  children hired by, 81–83
  educational benefits granted by, 83–85
  gifts and leasebacks by, 89–90
  partnerships, 85–87
  S corporations and ordinary corporations, 86, 87–89

Carl D. Perkins National Direct Student Loans (NDSL), 111
Certificates of Accrual on Treasury Securities (CATS), 42–43

certificates of deposit, 16, 28–30
charitable-remainder trusts, 75,
    80
checking accounts
    money-market funds used for,
        31
    NOW accounts and, 24–25
children
    borrowbacks between parents
        and, 64–65
    charitable-remainder trusts
        for, 75, 80
    Clifford trusts for, 68–69, 75,
        77–79, 87
    Crummey trusts for, 75, 79–
        80
    under 14, income shifting to,
        69, 70–72
    over 14, income shifting to,
        72
    hired by family-owned busi-
        nesses, 81–83
    Minors trusts for, 75–77
    as partners in businesses, 85–
        87
    trusts for, 73–80
    see also family; parents
Clifford trusts, 68–69, 75, 77–79,
    87
    Crummey trusts compared
        with, 79–80
closed-end unit trusts, 47
college costs
    certificates of deposit sched-
        uled for payments of, 29
    determining, 4–5, 133
    increase in, 1–2, 11–12
    need analysis for, 5–7, 72
    savings for, 13–20
CollegeCredit loans, 105
colleges
    loan programs of, 104–6
    Perkins loans, 111
    tuition plans of, 106–8
college savings bonds, 108–9

college students, taxable income
    of, 68
commercial paper, 16
common stocks, 50–52
    blue chip, 52
    dividends on, 51–52, 58, 81
    as gifts, 57–59
    growth, 52, 71–72
    inherited, 57
compound interest rates, 131–32
Connecticut Higher Education
    Supplemental Loan Authority,
    104
Consortium on Financing
    Higher Education, 105
corporate bonds, 48–50
    zero-coupon, 43–45
corporations, 86, 87–89
credit, lines of, 97–101
credit cards, 97
Crummey trusts, 75, 79–80
custodians (of minors' proper-
    ties), 61–62

debentures (corporate bonds),
    48
Depository Institutions Deregu-
    lation and Monetary Control
    Act (DIDMCA; U.S., 1980), 17
deregulation
    of banking, 17
    of financial world, 14–15
dividends, 51–52, 58, 71

educational-benefit trusts
    (EBTs), 84–85
educational fringe benefits, 83–
    85
educational loan programs, 97–
    99
Employee Retirement Act of
    1974, 91
Excel loans, 105

exemptions, on income taxes, 68
ExtraCredit Loans, 105, 111

family
    borrowing within, 64–65
    businesses owned by, 81–83
    gifts among, 55–56
    inheritances in, 56–57, 74
    planning for college costs by, 7–10, 113–26
    sales within, 60
    taxes on gifts within, 57–59
    see also children; parents
Federal Deposit Insurance Corporation (FDIC), 22–23
Federal Direct Student Loan Program, 111–12
Federal Family Education Loans Program
    Parent Loans for Undergraduate Students (PLUS), 12, 96, 105, 110–11
    Stafford Loans, 12, 105, 109–10
federal government
    financial aid from, 12
    loan programs, 109–12
    savings bonds from, 32–34, 70–71
    securities from agencies of, 37–39
    Stafford loans, 12, 105, 109–10
    Treasury bills, notes, and bonds from, 15, 16, 35–37, 41–43
Federal Home Loan Mortgage Corporation (Freddie Mac), 39
Federal Methodology, 6–7
Federal National Mortgage Association (Fannie Mae), 39
fees
    for certificates of deposit, 29

for common stocks, 51
for corporate bonds, 49
for government agency securities, 38
for home equity loans, 100
for life insurance policies, 54
for money-market deposit accounts, 26–27
for money-market funds, 31
for mortgage-backed securities, 40
for municipal bonds, 46
for NOW and Super-NOW accounts, 24–25
for passbook accounts, 23
for savings bonds (U.S.), 33
for Treasury bills, notes, and bonds, 35–36, 37
for zero-coupon municipal and corporate bonds, 44–45
for zero-coupon Treasury bonds, 42
fellowships
    as taxable income, 68
FICA (Federal Insurance Contributions Act), 83, 84
financial aid, 7–10
    college tuition plans as, 106–8
    disclosure of assets for, 72, 85
    family-owned businesses and, 81–83
    Higher Education Amendments and, 102–3
    loans as part of, 102–3
    need analysis for, 5–7, 72
    percentages of students receiving, 14
    students' assets in calculation of, 72
floating-rate municipal bonds, 47
Florida tuition plan, 107–8
401(k) plans, 93–94
FUTA (Federal Unemployment Tax Act), 83, 84

Garn-St Germain Depository Institutions Act (U.S., 1980), 17
general obligation bonds, 46
gifts, 55–65
borrowing within family and,
64–65
examples of, 57–59
from family-owned busi-
nesses, 89–90
inheritances, 56–57, 74
taxes on, 55–56, 59–60, 125,
129
Uniform Gifts to Minors Act
(state laws) on, 60–64, 76–
77
warnings on, 59–60
government. *see* federal government; state government
Government National Mortgage
Association (Ginnie Mae), 39,
41
grandparents, 58, 101, 123–25
grantor, 74–75
grants, 8
Pell grants, 110, 111
as taxable income, 68
growth stocks, 52, 71–72
guardians, 61

Higher Education Act of 1992,
110
Higher Education Amendments
(U.S., 1992), 102–3
Higher Education Services Corporation (New York State),
112
home equity loans, 99–101

income
from certificates of deposit,
29–30
of children under 14, 69, 70–
72
of children over 14, 72

from Clifford trusts, 75, 78
from common stocks, 51–52,
58, 71
from corporate bonds, 49–50
and educational attainment,
3–4, 95–96
from government agency securities, 39
inflation and, 13
from life insurance policies,
54
from money-market deposit
accounts, 27–28
from money-market funds,
31–32
from mortgage-backed securities, 40–41
from municipal bonds, 47–48
from NOW and Super-NOW
accounts, 25
from passbook accounts, 23–
24
from savings bonds, 34
of S corporations, 87–89
shrinking, 2
of students, taxation of, 68
from Treasury notes, bills, and
bonds, 36–37
from zero-coupon bonds, 43,
45
see also interest rates
income shifting and taxes, 67–
72
to children under 14, 69, 70–
72
to children over 14, 72
Clifford trusts for, 75, 77–79
Minors trusts for, 75–77
income taxes. *see* taxes
independent (Crummey) trusts,
75, 79–80
Individual Retirement Accounts
(IRAs), 53, 91–92
inflation, 1, 13
interest rates and, 14–15

municipal bonds and, 47–48
in planning for college, 4–5
Treasury bills, notes, bonds,
    and, 35
information sources on financial
    aid, 9
inheritances, 56–57
    as trusts, 74
Institutional Methodology, 6–7
insurance, 52–54, 71
interest-free loans, 64–65, 104
interest rates
    on certificates of deposit, 28,
        29–30
    compound, 131–32
    on corporate bonds, 49–50
    deregulation of, 17
    on government agency securi-
        ties, 39
    on home equity loans, 100
    inflation and, 14–15
    on life insurance policies, 54
    on loans from colleges, 104
    on loans within family, 64–65
    lower, impact of, 2
    on margin accounts, 101–2
    on money-market deposit ac-
        counts, 26, 27–28
    on money-market funds, 30,
        31–32
    on mortgage-backed securi-
        ties, 40–41
    on municipal bonds, 47–48
    on NOW and Super-NOW ac-
        counts, 24, 25
    on Parent Loan for Under-
        graduate Students (PLUS),
        110
    on passbook accounts, 23–24,
        97–98
    on passbook loans, 97–98
    on savings bonds (U.S.), 33,
        34
    simple, 131
Stafford loan program, 109

"teaser," 18
    on Treasury bills, notes, and
        bonds, 36–37, 43
    yields and, 131–32
    on zero-coupon municipal
        and corporate bonds, 45
investments
    in common stocks, 50–52
    in corporate bonds, 48–50
    in government agency securi-
        ties, 37–39
    held by children under 14, 69,
        70–72
    held by children over 14, 72
    held by Clifford trusts, 75, 78
    in Individual Retirement Ac-
        counts, 91–92
    in insurance, 52–54
    margin accounts for, 101–2
    in money-market funds, 16–
        17, 30–32
    in mortgage-backed securities,
        39–41
    in municipal bonds, 45–48
    under Prudent Man Rule, 61–
        62
    in Treasury bills, notes, and
        bonds, 35–37, 41–43
    in tuition plans, 106–8
    in zero-coupon municipal and
        corporate bonds, 43–45

junk bonds, 48

Keogh plans, 92–93

leasebacks, 89–90
legislation (U.S.)
    Depository Institutions Dereg-
        ulation and Monetary Con-
        trol Act, 17
    Higher Education Act of 1992,
        110

legislation (U.S.) *(continued)*
  Higher Education Amendments, 102–3
  Revenue Reconciliation Act of 1993, 67, 69–70
  Uniform Gifts to Minors Acts (state laws), 60–64, 76–77
  see also Tax Reform Act
life insurance, 52–54
lines of credit, 97–99
  home equity, 99–101
liquidity
  of certificates of deposit, 29
  of common stocks, 51
  of corporate bonds, 49
  of government agency securities, 38
  of life insurance policies, 54
  of money-market deposit accounts, 27
  of money-market funds, 31
  of mortgage-backed securities, 40
  of municipal bonds, 46–47
  of NOW and Super-NOW accounts, 25
  of passbook accounts, 23
  of savings bonds (U.S.), 33–34
  of Treasury bills, notes, and bonds, 36, 42–43
  of zero-coupon municipal and corporate bonds, 45
loans, 8
  from colleges, 104–6
  educational, 97–99
  within family, 64–65
  Federal Direct Student Loans, 111–12
  forgiveness of, for national service, 112
  home equity loans, 99–101
  income shifting and, 72
  interest-free, 64–65, 104
  on life insurance policies, 52–53, 54

Parent Loan for Undergraduate Students (PLUS), 12, 96, 105, 110–11
as part of financial aid, 102–3
passbook, 97–98
Perkins loans, 111
Stafford loan program, 12, 105, 109–10
from state agencies, 112

margin accounts, 101–2
M-CATS (Municipal Receipts), 44–45
men
  educational attainment and income of, 3–4
Michigan Education Trust, 107
Minors trusts, 75–77
money-market deposit accounts, 17–18, 26–28
  money-market funds compared with, 32
money-market funds, 16–17, 30–32
mortgage-backed securities, 39–41
municipal bonds, 45–48
  for income shifting, 43–45, 71
  tuition, 108–9
  zero-coupon, 43–45, 71
Municipal Receipts (M-CATS), 44–45
mutual funds
  federal agency, 39
  growth, 71–72
  money-market funds as, 16–17, 30–32
  municipal bond, 47

need analysis, 5–7, 72
negotiable orders of withdrawal (NOW) accounts, 24–25
New England Education Loan Marketing Association (Nellie Mae), 105

New York State Higher Education Service Corporation, 112
notes, Treasury, 35–37
NOW (negotiable orders of withdrawal) accounts, 24–25

ordinary corporations, 86, 87–89

Parent Loan for Undergraduate Students (PLUS), 12, 96, 105, 110–11
parents
  borrowbacks between children and, 64–65
  Clifford trusts established by, 68–69, 75, 77–79, 87
  and college loan programs, 104–6
  Minors trusts established by, 75–77
  Parent Loan for Undergraduate Students (PLUS), 12, 96, 105, 110–11
  tuition prepayment plans for, 106–8
  Uniform Gifts to Minors Acts (state laws) and, 60–64, 76–77
  see also children; family
partnerships, 85–87
passbook accounts, 22–24, 97–98
passbook loans, 97–98
pass-throughs (mortgage-backed securities), 39–41
Pell grants, 110, 111
pension plans, borrowing from, 90–94
Perkins loans, 111
planning for college costs, 1–10, 113–26
  by divorced mothers, 116–18
  economy and, 1–4

by grandparents, 58, 101, 123–25
by independent businessmen, widowed, 120–21
by independent professionals, 121–23
key factors in, 125
purpose of, 4–10
savings in, 10, 125
by young families, 114–16
by young professionals with two incomes, 118–19
private colleges
  cost of attending, 13–14
  increase in costs for, 11–12
  students receiving financial aid at, 14
property
  as gift, 57–59
  held by Clifford trusts, 75, 78
  Uniform Gifts to Minors Acts (state laws) on gifts of, 62–64
Prudent Man Rule, 61–62
public colleges
  cost of attending, 13–14
  increase in costs for, 11–12
  students receiving financial aid at, 14
"put" bonds, 47–48

qualified S trusts, 88

recession of 1990–1992, 2, 100
remaindermen, 74–75, 79
retirement plans, borrowing from, 90–94
revenue bonds, 46
Revenue Reconciliation Act of 1993, 67, 69–70
reverse annuity mortgages, 101
risks
  in certificates of deposit, 28
  in common stocks, 50–51
  in corporate bonds, 48–49

risk *(continued)*
  in government agency securities, 38
  in life insurance policies, 53–54
  in money-market deposit accounts, 26, 27
  in money-market funds, 30–31
  in mortgage-backed securities, 40
  in municipal bonds, 46
  in NOW and Super-NOW accounts, 24
  in passbook accounts, 22–23
  in savings accounts, 22–23
  in savings bonds (U.S.), 33
  in Treasury bills, notes, and bonds, 35, 41, 42
  in zero-coupon municipal and corporate bonds, 44
rule of 72, 132

safety
  of certificates of deposit, 28
  of common stocks, 50–51
  of corporate bonds, 48–49
  of government agency securities, 38
  of life insurance policies, 53–54
  of money-market deposit accounts, 26, 27
  of money-market funds, 30–31
  of mortgage-backed securities, 40
  of municipal bonds, 46
  of NOW and Super-NOW accounts, 24
  of passbook accounts, 22–23
  of savings bonds (U.S.), 33
  of Treasury bills, notes, and bonds, 35, 41, 42

  of zero-coupon municipal and corporate bonds, 44
salary-reduction [401(k)] plans, 93–94
savings, 13–20
  in certificates of deposit, 28–30
  in common stocks, 50–52
  complexities of, 14–18
  in corporate bonds, 48–50
  in government agency securities, 37–39
  in insurance, 52–54
  in money-market deposit accounts, 26–28
  in money-market funds, 30–32
  in mortgage-backed securities, 39–41
  in municipal bonds, 43–48
  in NOW and Super-NOW accounts, 24–25
  in passbook accounts, 22–24
  planning for, 10, 125
  risks and, 18
  in savings bonds (U.S.), 32–34
  in Treasury bills, notes, and bonds, 35–37, 41–43
  in zero-coupon bonds, 41–45
savings accounts, 22–24
  certificates of deposit, 16, 28–30
  lines of credit, 97–99
  money-market deposit accounts, 17–18, 26–28, 32
  NOW and Super-NOW, 24–25
  risks and rewards in, 22–23
savings bonds (U.S.), 32–34
  for income shifting, 70–71
scholarships, 8
  as taxable income, 68
S corporations, 86, 87–89
second mortgages, 99–101
securities
  Federal, trading, 36

government agency, 37–39
mortgage-backed, 39–41
Separate Trading of Registered
Interest and Principle of
Securities (STRIPS), 42–43
Share loans, 105
shares (common stocks), 50–52
in family-owned businesses,
transferred to children, 88–89
as gifts, 57–59
growth, 52, 71–72
inherited, 57
simple interest rates, 131
single-premium life insurance
policies, 53
speculative stocks, 52
spousal remainder trusts, 79
Stafford Loans, 12, 105, 109–10
state government
baccalaureate bonds, 108–9
depository institution insurance, 22–23
financial aid from, 12
student loan programs, 112
Uniform Gifts to Minors Act,
60–64, 76–77
stocks
blue-chip, 52
common, 50–52, 57–59, 71–
72, 81
in family-owned businesses,
transferred to children, 88–89
as gifts, 57–59
growth, 52, 71–72
inherited, 57
margin accounts for, 101–2
see also investments
straight life insurance policies,
52–54
Student Loan Marketing Association (Sallie Mae), 105
students, taxable income of, 68
Super-NOW (negotiable orders

of withdrawal) accounts,
24–25
Supplemental Educational Opportunity Grant (SEOG),
111

tax brackets, 67–68
taxes
borrowing within family and,
64–65
on businesses, 82
on charitable-remainder
trusts, 75, 80
Crummey trusts and, 75, 79–80
current income tax rates, 127–28
on gifts, 55–56, 59–60, 125,
129
income shifting and, 67–72,
125
on inheritances, 56–57
on interest, 15, 34
Keogh plans and, 93
on life insurance benefits, 54
Minors trusts and, 75–77
on municipal bonds, 43–44,
45, 47–48
salary-reduction plans and,
93–94
on savings bonds, 70–71
on transfers of business income, 89
and Treasury zero-coupon
bonds, 43
on trusts, 130
under Uniform Gifts to Minors
Acts (state laws), 63
Tax Reform Act (U.S., 1986)
below-market loans under,
104
borrowbacks under, 64–65
Clifford trusts under, 75, 77–79

Tax Reform Act (U.S., 1986)
(continued)
educational fringe benefits
and, 83–85
gifts under, 57–58
home equity loans under, 99
income shifting under, 67–72
inheritances under, 56–57
tax rates under, 127–28
trusts under, 73–74
term life insurance, 53
transaction costs. *see* fees
Treasury bills, 15, 16, 35–37
Treasury bonds, 35–37, 41–43
Treasury Investment Growth
Receipts (TIGRs), 42–43
Treasury notes, 35–37
trustees, 61, 74–75
of Clifford trusts, 75, 77–79
of Crummey trusts, 79–80
of Minors trusts, 75–77
of partnerships, 87
trusts, 61, 73–80
charitable-remainder trusts,
75, 80
Clifford trusts, 68–69, 75, 77–
79, 87
Crummey trusts, 75, 79–80
current income tax rates for,
130
educational-benefit trusts, 84–
85
leasebacks under, 89–90

Minors trusts, 75–77
qualified S trusts, 88
types of, 74
tuition bonds, 108–9
tuition-futures programs, 107–8
tuition plans, 106–8
tuition prepayment plans, 106–8

Uniform Gifts to Minors Acts
(state laws), 60–64, 76–77
U.S. savings bonds, 32–34, 70–
71

variable-rate insurance policies,
53, 54

whole-life insurance policies,
52–54
women
educational attainment and
income of, 3–4
worksheets, 133–40
work-study programs, 8

yield curves, 36–37

zero-coupon bonds
baccalaureate bonds, 108–9
municipal and corporate, 43–
45, 71, 107–9
Treasury, 41–43
in tuition-futures programs,
107–8